Functionall 1

TEACHER EDITION

Fiona Bramble

Functionall Books

www.eslenglish.ca

PUBLISHED BY FUNCTIONALL BOOKS
160 Eberts St.
Victoria B.C. Canada V8S 3H7

Functionall Books
www.eslenglish.ca

First published 2006

Printed In Canada

ISBN 978-0-9781142-0-6

Thanks and Acknowledgements

For all my former and current colleagues, an incredibly creative and motivated crew, who are generally overworked and underpaid. While I can do little about the latter, I hope this text can ease the burden of the former!
&
For my husband, Eric, and beautiful sons, Kieran and Truman, constant inspirations

Thanks to:

Elvira Perrella and Kristina Roach, for their patient and thorough editing
Doug Lovett, for his generous piloting and testing

Thanks also to authors and publishers and others who have given permission to reproduce text or other copyright work:

Universal Press Syndicate:	"Cathy"
	"Calvin"
	"Non Sequitur"
Big Stock Photos:	text photography

Thanks to authors who have provided excerpts and inspiration for activities:

Sharon Bertsch McGrayne:	*365 Surprising Scientific Facts, Breakthroughs and Discoveries*
Dr. John Gray:	*Men Are From Mars, Women Are From Venus* and *What Your Mother Didn't Know and Your Father Couldn't Tell You*
Dr. Edward M. Hallowell	"Are You Connected?"

In case of any omission, I express my apologies and welcome information from copyright sources

Introduction

This book is intended as a resource for all ESL/EFL teachers, green, expert, and everything in between. Some considerations before you leap in:

LANGUAGE: The vocabulary and gambits in this book are drawn primarily from a North American English lexicon. That said, there may be some lexical items that are not used in your region or country. Those items which, to the writer, seem to be regional or slang have been placed at the bottom of the lexical lists so that teachers can "white out" inappropriate items and perhaps add their own region-specific vocabulary.

PEDAGOGY: The book starts from the basic premise that the communicative approach to language acquisition contributes to a dynamic classroom, engaged learners and efficient, practical development of the target language. The text's approach embraces the notion that familiar and relevant contextual environments for language practice allow the learner to incorporate and acquire language "blocks" that may be otherwise overwhelming. The situational contexts herein are intended to be relevant, yet universal, current, yet timeless. The variety of activities and contexts allows for fun repetition of simple to sophisticated language structures.

LEVEL: This is a multi-level text which essentially ranges from intermediate to advanced. Teachers can easily modify exercises to make them suitable for their particular levels or choose only some activities from each unit as is appropriate. Vocabulary that may be challenging is underlined in every activity in order for teachers to pre- or post-teach items when necessary.

KEY: Each unit includes a key which provides extra information or suggestions connected to a particular context or function:

Δ   CHALLENGES:
students tend to have difficulty with the grammar structure of particular items. Consider pre-teaching or, if level-inappropriate, avoiding these structures.
◊   GRAMMAR EXPANSION:
suggestions for grammar structures that match the context or gambits well.
O   PRONUNCIATION:
considerations for incidental pronunciation practice

HOMEWORK: The Homework Book can be purchased separately from this text. It is a speaking and journal notebook for each student to keep and provides another assessment tool for teachers. It offers suggestions for out-of-class speaking practice and writing reinforcement. With The Homework Book, each student is able to keep a record of their language experiences; however, each unit in this text also offers alternative homework ideas.

Contents

BREAKING UP AND MAKING UP

It's not you, it's me   I'M NOT INTO ANYTHING SERIOUS RIGHT NOW

PEOPLE CHANGE   **our lifestyles are too different**

I'm just not ready   you're too good for me   I need some space

I JUST DON'T HAVE THE TIME FOR A RELATIONSHIP

Dear John,

we're going in different directions

I NEVER SEE YOU ANYMORE

I'M NOT THE ONE FOR YOU   *I think we should take a break*

I am not in love with you anymore   ***There's somebody else***

I'll change   *is it me?*   **WHO IS SHE/HE?**

DON'T GO!   but you said you loved me...

Will you call me?   Can we be friends?

I don't want to be without you

I DON'T UNDERSTAND

IT'S YOUR LOSS   I don't want to be just your friend

Can we talk about this?   *GIVE ME ANOTHER CHANCE*

I'd like to try again   PLEASE FORGIVE ME

I'll make it up to you   **I can't believe I almost lost you**

I WAS SUCH A JERK

I don't know what I was thinking

You're the best thing that ever happened to me

I WAS LOST WITHOUT YOU   **will you take me back?**

I never want to fight with you again

BREAKING UP AND MAKING UP: *JIGSAW*

CONVERSATION A: BREAKING UP

A	CAN WE TALK?
B	OF COURSE. WHAT'S UP?
A	YOU'RE SUCH AN AWESOME GUY BUT I FEEL LIKE <u>I NEED SOME SPACE.</u>
B	<u>I DON'T UNDERSTAND.</u> I THOUGHT THINGS WERE GREAT.
A	I JUST THINK <u>WE SHOULD TAKE A LITTLE BREAK.</u>
B	<u>IS IT ME?</u> IS IT SOMETHING I'VE DONE?
A	NO. NO. <u>IT'S NOT YOU. IT'S ME.</u> <u>I'M JUST NOT READY.</u>
B	BUT <u>YOU SAID YOU LOVED ME.</u>
A	<u>PEOPLE CHANGE.</u> I HOPE WE CAN BE FRIENDS.
B	<u>I DON'T WANT TO BE JUST YOUR FRIEND.</u>
A	I'M SORRY. <u>I'M NOT THE ONE FOR YOU.</u>
B	WELL <u>IT'S YOUR LOSS!</u>

from *Function-all 1 Intermediate Plus* by Fiona Bramble © Functionall Books 2006 www.eslenglish.ca

BREAKING UP AND MAKING UP: *JIGSAW*

CONVERSATION B: MAKING UP

A	HEY, HOW HAVE YOU BEEN?
B	I'M SURVIVING.
A	I'M NOT. I MISS YOU SO MUCH. <u>I WAS SUCH A JERK.</u> CAN YOU <u>FORGIVE ME</u>?
B	IT'S NOT THAT EASY.
A	<u>I DON'T KNOW WHAT I WAS THINKING. YOU'RE THE BEST THING THAT EVER HAPPENED TO ME.</u>
B	YOU SHOULD HAVE THOUGHT OF THAT BEFORE!
A	<u>PLEASE GIVE ME ANOTHER CHANCE.</u>
B	I JUST DON'T KNOW.
A	<u>I'LL MAKE IT UP TO YOU.</u> I PROMISE!
B	ALL RIGHT. I HAVE MISSED YOU.
A	<u>I WAS LOST WITHOUT YOU.</u>
B	ME TOO. <u>I NEVER WANT TO FIGHT WITH YOU AGAIN.</u>

from *Function-all 1 Intermediate Plus* by Fiona Bramble © Functionall Books 2006   www.eslenglish.ca

BREAKING UP AND MAKING UP

Discussion questions:
In pairs or small groups, discuss the following:

1. At what stage (beginning, breaking up, making up, over…) is the woman's (Cathy) romantic relationship in the above comic strip? Why does Cathy say something different to each person?

2. In serious relationships, do you think women want men to change? If so, what are some typical things women want men to change?

3. Do you think men want women to change? If so, in what way?

4. Have you ever <u>broken up with</u> someone? Has someone ever broken up with you?

5. When was the last time you comforted a friend who had been <u>dumped</u>? How did you make him/her feel better?

6. It is said that "breaking up is hard to do". What is hard about <u>making up?</u>

7. Are you the type of person who can <u>forgive and forget</u> easily or do you <u>hold a grudge</u>?

8. When did you last have to <u>swallow your pride</u> to <u>smooth over</u> a situation?

9. Do you believe in <u>soulmates</u>? Is there only one soulmate for each person?

10. Who, in your life, is the <u>one who got away</u>?

I JUST DON'T KNOW YOU ANYMORE...
Breaking up and making up in relationships and life

<u>Function Practice:</u>

1. **In a small group or with a partner, discuss and match the "breaking up" expressions with a situation below. There may be more than one correct answer! Explain your choices.**

> A   I NEED SOMETHING A LITTLE MORE CHALLENGING
> B   WE'RE GOING IN DIFFERENT DIRECTIONS
> C   I JUST NEVER SEE YOU ANYMORE
> D   THERE'S SOMEBODY ELSE
> E   OUR LIFESTYLES ARE TOO DIFFERENT
> F   I WANT TO DO SOME STUFF <u>ON MY OWN</u> FOR A WHILE
> G   I JUST CAN'T <u>KEEP UP</u>
> H   I'M NOT INTO ANYTHING SERIOUS RIGHT NOW

1. ____ a job

2. ____ a team

3. ____ a business partnership

4. ____ a <u>fling</u>

5. ____ a marriage

6. ____ a roommate

7. ____ a friendship

8. ____ a band

2. **With a partner, use "Breaking up and Making up" to act out (role play) the following situations. Use as many different expressions as you can!**

#1	PARTNER A:	You have become unhappy in your job and approach your boss to give him/her your <u>resignation</u>.
	PARTNER B:	Your top employee tells you he/she is leaving the company. You are shocked and do not want him/her to leave.

#2	PARTNER A:	One of your good friends just told you that you are a <u>lousy</u> friend because you never call him/her. He/she thinks that <u>it's not worth</u> making the effort to be your friend anymore.
	PARTNER B:	You are angry with a good friend because he/she hardly ever calls you. You tell him/her that you don't want to be friends anymore but you really just want him or her to <u>hang out with</u> you more often.

#3	PARTNER A:	You've been dating several people <u>off and on</u> for the last few months and have fallen in love with one of them. You have to tell one of your *other* dates that you don't want to see him/her anymore.
	PARTNER B:	You've been dating someone for the last few months and you are <u>head over heels</u> in love with him/her. You think he/she might be "the one" and you think he/she feels the same way about you.

#4	PARTNER A:	Your husband or wife is <u>giving you the cold shoulder</u>. The two of you had a big argument last night but you think she/he should apologize for the things she/he said to you.
	PARTNER B:	Your husband or wife is <u>giving you the cold shoulder</u>. The two of you had a big argument last night but you think she/he should apologize for the things she/he said to you.

3. **Choose your favorite role play and spend 2-3 minutes acting it out for another pair or in front of the class. Try to remember as many "breaking up and making up" expressions as you can. Don't look at your "Breaking up and Making up" sheet!**

<u>Homework:</u>

A. "Speaking" and "Journal" activities from <u>The Homework Book</u>
OR

B. Ask a native speaker (homestay family/friend/another teacher) about their first love and who broke up with whom!

♪ baby, come back ♫

Songs about <u>Breaking up</u>

"THE CLICHÉ BREAKUP SONG"* | **"SONG FOR THE DUMPED"***
MISTER STICK | **BEN FOLDS FIVE**

BABY
WE NEED _____
WHY DON'T I COME OVER TO YOUR
PLACE TONIGHT
CUZ THERE'S SOMETHING I NEED TO
TELL YOU

WE'VE BEEN THROUGH SO MUCH
TOGETHER
WE SURE HAD OUR UPS AND _____
TIMES ARE CHANGING
WE'RE GROWING _____

LET'S JUST BE _____
CUZ IT'S NOT _____, IT'S _____
I REALLY NEED SOME _____ RIGHT NOW
BABY CAN'T YOU SEE

I SWEAR THAT THERE'S _____ ELSE
SHE MEANT _____ TO ME
BEFORE I CAN BE OK WITH US
I'VE GOT TO BE _____ WITH ME

YOU BE JUST _____WITHOUT ME BABY
THERE'S PLENTY OF FISH _____

SO YOU WANTED TO
TAKE _____
SLOW IT _____ SOME, AND HAVE
SOME _____

WELL F**K YOU TOO
GIVE ME MY _____ BACK
GIVE ME MY _____BACK, YOU B****H
I WANT MY _____ BACK

AND DON'T FORGET
AND DON'T FORGET TO GIVE ME BACK
MY BLACK T-SHIRT

I WISH I HADN'T BOUGHT
YOU DINNER
RIGHT BEFORE
YOU _____ ME
ON YOUR FRONT PORCH

---

* These lyrics represent excerpts only

<u>Function Practice</u>:

1. **Thinking about the context and some of the expressions from "Breaking up and Making up", try to guess, with a partner, the missing words from the songs above.**

2. For fun, say the expressions to your partner as if you were in that situation!

3. Compare your answers with another pair. Your teacher will give you the correct answers.

4. With your partner, write one verse of your own break-up or make-up song. If you are brave enough, sing it to the class!

_____

_____

_____

_____

_____

_____

Post-Discussion:

In small groups or with a partner, discuss the following:

1. Do you think a man or woman would sing the songs above? Why?
2. How are the perspectives of the two songs different?
3. Why is the song by Mister Stick called "The **Cliché** Breakup Song"?
4. Which song do you identify with more? Why?
5. Have you ever listened to breakup songs? If so, how did they make you feel? Do you have a favorite depressing song ☺ ?

Homework:

A. "Speaking" or "Journal" activities from **The Homework Book**
                          OR
B. Go on the Internet or listen to the radio for a love or breakup song in ENGLISH. Try to listen for some of the expressions you've studied.

Key:

O	you're <u>too</u> good for me
O	**SOMETHING <u>JUST</u> DOESN'T FEEL RIGHT**
O	*I'm <u>just</u> not ready*
O2	***There<u>'s</u> somebody <u>else</u>***
O2	I <u>am not in</u> love with you anymore
O2	we're going <u>in</u> different directions
O2	**I'M NOT INTO ANYTHING SERIOUS RIGHT NOW**
O/O2	I don't <u>want to</u> be <u>just</u> your friend
O3	I don't <u>want to</u> be without you
O2	*<u>is it</u> me?*
O3	***I never <u>want to</u> fight with you again***
O2	*I'll <u>make it up to</u> you*
O2/O3	**I can't believe <u>I</u> almost lost <u>you</u>**
O2/O3	I'd like to try again

Δ CHALLENGES:

ALL   Assisting students with contextual appropriateness and pronunciation is often necessary

◇ GRAMMAR EXPANSION:

ALL (BREAKING UP & BEGGING*)   Practice with simple present or present progressive

MAKING UP   Practice with "will" for future promises

O PRONUNCIATION:

O   Students neglect to stress the "just" and "too"

O2   Students struggle with the consonant-vowel linking patterns

O3   Students neglect to make the correct reduction,

e.g. "want to" → /wɔːnə/

"lost you" → /lɔːstʃyə/

ALL   Students should be encouraged to practice sentence stress and intonation patterns

*or whatever "title" your class gives to the second section!

from *Function-all 1 Intermediate Plus* by Fiona Bramble © Functionall Books 2006   www.eslenglish.ca

The <u>complete</u> songs from context2:

a.   The underlined words are the missing (cloze) items

b.   The bold words represent the students' excerpts

c.   The italicized words represent the omitted verses

THE CLICHÉ BREAKUP SONG MISTER STICK	SONG FOR THE DUMPED BEN FOLDS FIVE
BABY WE NEED <u>TO TALK</u> WHY DON'T I COME OVER TO YOUR PLACE TONIGHT CUZ THERE'S SOMETHING I NEED TO TELL YOU	SO YOU WANTED TO TAKE <u>A BREAK</u> SLOW IT <u>DOWN</u> SOME, AND HAVE SOME <u>SPACE</u>
WE'VE BEEN THROUGH SO MUCH TOGETHER WE SURE HAD OUR UPS AND <u>DOWNS</u> TIMES ARE CHANGING WE'RE GROWING <u>APART</u>	WELL FUCK YOU TOO GIVE ME MY <u>MONEY</u> BACK GIVE ME MY <u>MONEY</u> BACK, YOU BITCH I WANT MY <u>MONEY</u> BACK
LET'S JUST BE <u>FRIENDS</u> CUZ IT'S NOT <u>YOU</u>, IT'S <u>ME</u> I REALLY NEED SOME <u>SPACE</u> RIGHT NOW BABY CAN'T YOU SEE	AND DON'T FORGET AND DON'T FORGET TO GIVE ME BACK MY BLACK T-SHIRT
I SWEAR THAT THERE'S <u>NO ONE</u> ELSE SHE MEANT <u>NOTHING</u> TO ME BEFORE I CAN BE OK WITH US I'VE GOT TO BE <u>OK</u> WITH ME	I WISH I HADN'T BOUGHT YOU DINNER RIGHT BEFORE YOU <u>DUMPED</u> ME ON YOUR FRONT PORCH
JUST ONE LAST KISS GOODBYE SHOULD I SPEND THE NIGHT?	*GIVE ME MY MONEY BACK GIVE ME MY MONEY BACK, YOU BITCH I WANT MY MONEY BACK AND DON'T FORGET AND DON'T FORGET TO GIVE ME BACK MY BLACK T-SHIRT*
LET'S JUST BE FRIENDS CUZ IT'S NOT YOU, IT'S ME I REALLY NEED SOME SPACE RIGHT NOW BABY CAN'T YOU SEE	*SO YOU WANTED TO TAKE A BREAK SLOW IT DOWN SOME, AND HAVE SOME SPACE*
I SWEAR THAT THERE'S NO ONE ELSE SHE MEANT NOTHING TO ME BEFORE I CAN BE OK WITH US I'VE GOT TO BE OK WITH ME	*GIVE ME MY MONEY BACK GIVE ME MY MONEY BACK, YOU BITCH I WANT MY MONEY BACK I WANT MY MONEY BACK AND DON'T FORGET...*
YOU BE JUST FINE WITHOUT ME BABY THERE'S PLENTY OF FISH <u>IN THE SEA</u>	

from *Function-all I Intermediate Plus* by Fiona Bramble © Functionall Books 2006   www.eslenglish.ca

TEACHER'S PAGES

Teaching Ideas:

1gambits

✓ elicit gambits from students prior to handing out gambit sheet; have a contest to see which team guesses the most from the list

✓ copy pictures separately onto an overhead transparency and have a brief class discussion about what is happening in each

✓ attempt to "title" each different section, e.g. "breaking up", "begging" ☺, "making up"

2warm-up

✓ cut "jigsaw" into strips, mix them up, and have pairs or teams race to put conversations in correct order (there may be more than one correct order; be flexible!)

✓ write each "line" in large letters on separate cards and tape or attach to the front of each student. Have teams or entire class try to physically place themselves in the correct order

✓ ensure students practice conversation in pairs for introduction and reinforcement

3discussion

✓ pre-teach underlined vocabulary if necessary. Students can use drawing activities, charades, magazine scavenger hunts, etc... to guess or demonstrate meaning

✓ cut questions into strips and a) post them around the class or school for a "run-read-ask" relay or b) put the strips in a bag or basket or c) do a "strip-exchange", in which students each have one question and, after asking one student, exchange questions with him/her and move on to another student. Repeat until everyone has heard and asked almost all questions

✓ copy comic strip onto overhead transparency for class discussion. Note: students may not understand the expression "That'll be the day!"

context1

✓ #1 could be done on an overhead with choices covered for greater challenge and discussion

context2

✓ bring in recordings of songs or have students listen to them on the computer/Internet

✓ do a listening cloze with songs

✓ give each student a line in one of the songs and ask them to stand up, sing, or wave (or all three!) when they hear it

checking understanding

Do you follow?   *IS THIS TOO TECHNICAL FOR YOU?*

Got it?   Am I making any sense?   *Do you catch my drift?*

Am I talking too fast?   Any questions?

Are you with me so far?   (Does it) make sense?

Are you familiar with____?   **So far, so good?**

DO YOU GET THE GIST?   Do I need to elaborate?

Do you understand?   You know what I mean?

Are you following me?   Do you want me to slow down?

confirming and clarifying information

SO WHAT YOU'RE SAYING IS (THAT) ____

If I understand you correctly, then ____   *Do you mean ____?*

Are you suggesting (that) ____?   **Do you mean to say (that) ____?**

I'M NOT SURE I FULLY UNDERSTAND WHAT YOU ARE SAYING.

What are you getting at?   Could you explain ____ a little further?

Could you elaborate on ____?   I'm not sure what you mean by ____

What the heck are you talking about?   **Could you back up a bit?**

This is way over my head!   If I'm hearing you correctly, then____

what I think you're saying is (that) _____

CHECKING UNDERSTANDING & CONFIRMING & CLARIFYING INFORMATION: IDIOM & VOCABULARY QUIZ

#1   When someone says, "Are you following me?", you should say:
- A.   No, I was just window-shopping
- B.   Yes, I thought you were a former roommate who owes me money
- C.   Yes, I think so.   OR   No, not really.

#2   If you are "with someone", you are:
- A.   on a date or hanging out with him/her
- B.   understanding what they are saying
- C.   both A and B

#3   "So far, so good" means:
- A.   Everything is o.k. at this point
- B.   I love to travel
- C.   I don't mind walking long distances

#4   If you "get the gist", you:
- A.   should see a doctor right away
- B.   understand the general idea
- C.   are being honoured

#5   You would want someone to "elaborate" if he/she said:
- A.   I had this great quantum physics class today!
- B.   I think I have a *wedgie!
- C.   I've got some great news!

#6   When you "catch someone's drift", you:
- A.   understand the general idea
- B.   need a good glove
- C.   should plug your nose

#7   If you don't know what someone is "getting at", it's important to:
- A.   give him/her a ride
- B.   ask him/her to explain
- C.   get him/her a ladder

*a "wedgie" occurs when one's underwear is uncomfortably higher than it is intended to be

from *Function-all I Intermediate Plus* by Fiona Bramble © Functionall Books 2006   www.eslenglish.ca

CHECKING UNDERSTANDING &
CONFIRMING & CLARIFYING INFORMATION

CALVIN AND HOBBES © 1993 Watterson. Dist. By UNIVERSAL PRESS SYNDICATE. Reprinted with permission. All rights reserved.

Discussion Questions:

In pairs or small groups, discuss the following:

1. What does "Calvin" suggest is happening to language? What does "Hobbes" suggest this change might mean for comprehension?

2. What more polite question could Hobbes use instead of "What?" (Check your "Checking Understanding" expressions!) Is "what?" acceptable in casual conversation?

3. Do you <u>assume</u> people understand what you are saying most of the time or do you often check if they are <u>following</u> you?

4. When you are in class, do think it's important to understand every detail or is <u>the gist</u> enough? Explain.

5. What kinds of <u>non-verbal</u> clues do we give to show we do or do not understand someone? Show your partner!

6. Does it annoy you when people finish your sentences for you? Why do people do this?

7. Are you comfortable asking *anybody* (a professor, a parent, a doctor...) for clarification when you don't understand something? Why or why not?

8. Do people in this culture or in your culture <u>beat around the bush</u> more? Why do you think this is so?

9. Do you tend to <u>go off on a tangent</u> when talking? How do you feel when others go off on a tangent?

10. Say: G-O-C-H-Y-A (/gɔːtʃyə/) really loudly. What does it mean?

HEY, HOW DID YOU GET THAT BILATERAL PROBITA HEMATOMA*?

Checking, confirming, and clarifying "Jargon"

Pre-Discussion:

In small groups or with a partner, discuss the following:

1. What is the difference between *slang* and *jargon*?
2. Are *slang* and *jargon* count, or noncount nouns? ☺
3. How is *jargon* useful? Problematic?
4. What professionals/workers use *jargon* with each other but layman's terms with the public? HINT: see page heading above!
5. What are three examples of jargon your teacher has used today?

Function Practice:

1. **With a partner, match the *jargon* below with its field or profession:**

   1. PINCH HITTER _____   A. PHOTOGRAPHY

   2. AFFECTIVE FILTER _____   B. POETRY

   3. HEROIC COUPLET _____   C. LANGUAGE LEARNING

   4. APPENDECTOMY _____   D. BASEBALL

   5. APERTURE _____   E. MEDICINE

2. **Explain to each other, if you can, the meanings of the words on the left in layman's terms. Your teacher will help you. Use your "Checking Understanding and Confirming and Clarifying Information" expressions.**

*a "bilateral probita hematoma" is what is commonly known as a "black eye" or a "shiner" (slang)

3. On your own, spend approximately 10 minutes thinking about your major, field of interest, <u>area of expertise</u>, special talent, or hobby. *Write down* at least 3 examples of jargon unique to that field, including at least 1 process, theory, or technique. You CAN use your dictionary (and your teacher!)

e.g.   COOKING

JARGON:
1. blanch
PROCESS/THEORY/TECHNIQUE:
Name: Blanch **Brief explanation:** To place foods in boiling water briefly either to partially cook them or to aid in the removal of the skin (i.e. nuts, peaches, tomatoes).

MY TOPIC:

JARGON:
1.
2.
3.
PROCESS/THEORY/TECHNIQUE:
Name: Brief explanation:

3. When you and your partner are *both* ready, introduce your topics and explain your jargon and processes. Use as many of the expressions from "Checking Understanding and Confirming and Clarifying Information" as you can to make sure you have understood each other. If there is time, explain *your partner's* topic to a new partner.

<u>Homework:</u>

A. "Speaking" and "Journal" activities from <u>The Homework Book</u>
OR

B. Repeat #3 and #4 above with a native speaker and report to the class.

HONEY, WHAT ARE YOU THINKING ABOUT?
Checking, confirming, and clarifying gender mysteries

Pre-activity:

1. Your teacher or a classmate is going to read the following short passage aloud. Do not read it at the same time; just close your eyes and listen!

> "Men mistakenly expect women to think, communicate, and react the way men do; women mistakenly expect men to feel, communicate, and <u>respond</u> the way women do. We have forgotten that men and women are supposed to be different. As a result our relationships are filled with unnecessary <u>friction</u> and <u>conflict</u>"
> (from <u>Men are from Mars, Women are from Venus</u>, John Gray, Ph.D)

2. When your teacher or classmate has finished, turn to the person beside you and talk for 5-10 minutes about:

a. whether you agree or disagree with the statement
b. your own experiences in connection to the statement
c. anything the statement makes you think of!

3. Share some of your ideas with the rest of the class.

Function Practice:

1. With your partner (better if your partner is of the opposite sex) or in a small group, discuss the short dialogue below:

She says:	He says:
"How was your day?"	"Fine"
She means:	**He means:**
"Let's talk. I'm interested in your day and I hope you are interested in mine"	"I am giving you a short answer because I need some time alone"

from <u>What Your Mother Couldn't Tell You & Your Father Didn't Know</u>, John Gray, Ph.D

Thinking about the dialogue above, finish these two sentences:

a. Women often want to...
b. Men sometimes...

2. With your partner or group, using your "Checking Understanding and Confirming and Clarifying Information" expressions, try to solve some of the following "gender mysteries":

    e.g.   Man: Why do WOMEN GO TO THE BATHROOM TOGETHER?

          Woman: So we can talk about guys. <u>Get it?</u>

          Man: <u>So what you're saying is that</u> women don't really have to "go" at all, they just want to talk?

MEN ASK WOMEN:

"Why do women …?" or "What do women mean when they say…?"

<u>DO:</u>

1. GOSSIP ABOUT OTHER WOMEN
2. SAY "NOTHING'S WRONG" WHEN SOMETHING IS
3. <u>PLAY HARD TO GET</u>
4.

<u>SAY:</u>

5. "DOES THIS MAKE ME LOOK FAT?"
6. "DO YOU FIND HER ATTRACTIVE?"
7. "WHAT ARE YOU THINKING?"
8.

---

* fill in the empty spaces with your own ideas!

WOMEN ASK MEN:

"Why do men …?" or "What do men mean when they say…?"

<u>DO:</u>

1. LEAVE THE TOILET SEAT UP
2. LOOK AT OTHER WOMEN
3. FORGET ANNIVERSARIES
4.

<u>SAY:</u>

5. "I LOVE YOU BUT I'M NOT IN LOVE WITH YOU"
6. "YOU LOOK FINE"
7. "I NEED A BEER"
8.

<u>Homework:</u>

    A. "Speaking" and "Journal" activities from <u>The Homework Book</u>

                            OR

    B. Ask a native speaker (homestay family/friend/another teacher) what he/she will never understand about the opposite sex.

Key:

O Do you follow?   O IS THIS TOO TECHNICAL FOR YOU?

O2 Got it?   O2 Am I making any sense?

O Do you catch my drift?   O2 Am I talking too fast?

O Are you with me so far?   Δ Are you familiar with_____?

O/ O2 DO YOU GET THE GIST?   O Do you understand?

O2 Do I need to elaborate?   O Are you following me?

O/O2 You know what I mean?   O Do you want me to slow down?

Δ CHALLENGES:

Δ   Students often neglect to use a gerund, noun phrase or clause following the preposition.

◊ GRAMMAR EXPANSION:

ALL   Practice with yes/no questions and short answers.

e.g. A: Am I making sense?

B: Yes, you are/No, you're not

O PRONUNCIATION:

O   In fast speech, "you" is often reduced to /yə/, particularly after "do" and "are" and "for"

O2   Some students struggle with consonant-vowel linking patterns and reduction

ALL   Some students neglect question intonation patterns

◊/ O2 SO WHAT YOU'RE SAYING IS (THAT) ___

◊/O Do you mean ____?   ◊/O Are you suggesting (that) _____?

◊/O Do you mean to say (that) ____?   O2 What are you getting at?

O2 I'M NOT SURE I FULLY UNDERSTAND WHAT YOU ARE SAYING.

O /O2 Could you explain ___ a little further?

O /O2 Could you elaborate on ___? O/O2 I'm not sure what you mean by _____

O/O2 What the heck are you talking about?   O/O2 Could you back up a bit?

◊/O2 What I think you're saying is (that) _____

◊ GRAMMAR EXPANSION:

◊   Practice with noun clauses

e.g. What I think you are saying is that you love ice cream more than me!

O PRONUNCIATION:

O   In fast speech, "you" is often reduced to /yə/

O2   Some students struggle with consonant-vowel linking patterns and reduction

ALL   Some students neglect question intonation patterns

TEACHER'S PAGES

Teaching Ideas:

1gambits

- ✓ elicit gambits from students prior to handing out gambit sheet; have a contest to see which team guesses the most from the list.
- ✓ the idiomatic vocabulary is reviewed in **2warm-up**, so you may want to do the warm-up first before discussing use and meaning of gambits.

2warm-up

- ✓ quiz works well on an overhead; class can be broken up into teams and each team can "bet" (with fake money, coins, etc...) on what they think the right answer is.
- ✓ can be done in pairs and the pair with the most correct answers wins!

3discussion

- ✓ pre-teach underlined vocabulary if necessary. Students can use drawing activities, charades, magazine scavenger hunts, etc... to guess or demonstrate meaning.
- ✓ #1 & #2 can be placed on an overhead for pre-discussion.
- ✓ #3-10: cut questions into strips and a) post them around the class or school for a "run-read-ask" relay or b) put the strips in a bag or basket or c) do a "strip-exchange", in which students each have one question and, after asking one student, exchange questions with him/her and move on to another student. Repeat until everyone has heard and asked almost all questions.

context1

- ✓ "guess who" is in the picture (Prince Phillip).
- ✓ choose a few students for spontaneous speaking (3 minutes each) and ask them to explain how Prince Phillip got his "shiner" ☺.
- ✓ "matching" exercise can be cut up, glued onto cards, and used for a very quick game of "snap". (You will have to referee)

*DEFINITIONS:	
pinch hitter:	a substitute for a teammate at bat (BASEBALL)
affective filter:	motives, needs, attitudes, and emotions which affect the rate and quality of language learning (LANGUAGE LEARNING)
heroic couplet:	a rhyming couplet of iambic pentameter (POETRY) *Some foreign writers, some our own despise* *The ancients only, or the moderns, prize.* -Alexander Pope
appendectomy:	surgical removal of the appendix (MEDICINE)
aperture:	the size of the opening of a lens (PHOTOGRAPHY)

context2

- ✓ ensure students add their own ideas in the blank lines.
- ✓ "He Said, She Said" (with Kevin Bacon), though dated, and "What Women Want" (with Mel Gibson) are funny movies for follow-up and to review gambits post-viewing.

Initiating debate/discussion

- Why is/do __?
- I can't believe that __
- How do you feel about __?
- It's unbelievable that __
- Do you have a position on__?
- Where do you stand on__?
- What's your take on__?
- __ is a controversial topic.
- There's been a lot of controversy about__

Stating a position

- I feel strongly that__
- In my opinion, __
- I firmly believe that__
- I think it's good/bad that__
- I've always thought that__
- If you ask me, __
- There's no question that__
- I have to agree that__
- Without a doubt,
- Who can argue__?
- In my mind,
- Everybody knows that__

Concession *

- You've raised a valid point →
- It's true that__   →
- I hadn't thought of that   →

- I'll give you that   →
- That is a factor   →

- That's an interesting point →
- I'm willing to concede on that point

Rebuttal*

→Nonetheless, __
→yet, it is also true that__
→However, it doesn't change the fact that__
→although I still feel strongly that__
→but a more significant consideration is__
→Nevertheless, I believe that__

Disagreement

- I highly doubt that__
- I'm not sure that's an accurate assessment of the situation
- I don't think you're looking at the whole picture
- I think you've taken it out of context
- I think you have missed the point
- That's b.s.
- That doesn't make any sense

Summarizing and Concluding

- In brief,
- In short,
- To sum up,
- Summing up,
- My point is__
- In a nutshell,
- In conclusion,
- To wrap up,
- The bottom line is__
- When all is said and done,
- My final point is __
- All in all,

* a "concession" expression can be used on its own or paired with a "rebuttal" expression as the arrows indicate

Debate and Discussion

DEBATE AND DISCUSSION: *POSITION CARDS*

<u>I feel strongly that</u> dogs should be on a leash at all times anywhere	<u>In my opinion,</u> red lipstick looks really <u>sleazy</u>	<u>I firmly believe that</u> alcohol should be illegal	<u>I think it's bad that</u> parents lie to their children about Santa Claus
<u>I've always thought that</u> George W. Bush is a wise man	<u>If you ask me,</u> learning English is <u>overrated</u>	<u>There's no question that</u> money is the most important thing in life	<u>I have to agree that</u> "a fat tax" on airplanes is necessary
<u>Without a doubt,</u> Tom Cruise is the worst actor in Hollywood	<u>In my mind,</u> we'd be better off without computers	<u>Who can argue that</u> marijuana is a great way to relax?	<u>Everybody knows that</u> red meat is bad for you
<u>I feel strongly that</u> children should be <u>spanked</u>	<u>In my opinion,</u> basketball players should be paid more	<u>I firmly believe that</u> women should not work after marriage	<u>I think it's good that</u> Brad Pitt and Jennifer Aniston <u>split up.</u>
<u>I've always thought that</u> recycling is a waste of time	<u>If you ask me,</u> <u>Speedos</u> are sexy	<u>There's no question that</u> I look silly in a bikini	<u>I have to agree that</u> hunting animals is necessary
<u>Without a doubt,</u> dolphins are smarter than humans	<u>In my mind,</u> poetry is incredibly interesting	<u>Who can argue that</u> pizza is a healthy snack?	<u>Everybody knows that</u> "stealing" music from the Internet is <u>unethical</u>

DEBATE AND DISCUSSION: *CONCESSION/ DISAGREEMENT CARDS*

You've raised a valid point. concession	It's true (that)_____. concession	I hadn't thought of that! concession	I'll give you that. concession
That is a factor. concession	That's an interesting point. concession	I'm willing to concede on that point. concession	That's right! concession
I highly doubt that____. disagreement	I'm not sure that's an accurate assessment of the situation. d	I don't think you're looking at the whole picture. disagreement	I think you've taken it out of context. disagreement
I think you've missed the point. disagreement	That's b.s.! disagreement	What the heck are you talking about? disagreement	That doesn't make any sense. disagreement

Instructions:

1. Copy as many sets of "POSITION CARDS" as groups (4-6 students) in your class
2. Cut each set into separate squares and distribute to each group. Place the stack of cards face down in the center of the group
3. Each student should have 1 "CONCESSION CARD" and 1 "DISAGREEMENT CARD". Make as many copies as necessary (there are 8 of each in the set).
4. Taking turns, students in each group should select a "POSITION CARD" from the pile, read it aloud and attempt to convince the others in the group that they agree with the sentiment on the card.
5. After several minutes, the rest of the group "votes" on the argument by repeating either their "CONCESSION CARD" or "DISAGREEMENT CARD".
6. If there are more "CONCESSION" votes than "DISAGREEMENT" votes, the student "wins" his or her card. The student with the most "POSITION CARDS" at the end is the winner!

DEBATE AND DISCUSSION

"It is better to debate a question without settling it than to settle a question without debating it."

Joseph Joubert, French Philosopher (1809)

Discussion Questions:
In pairs or small groups, discuss the following:

1. What does the above quotation suggest about the purpose of "debate"? Do you agree with the above quotation? Why or why not?

2. Is there a difference between debate and argument? Explain.

3. What are some controversial subjects that you are <u>touchy</u> about? Why are you sensitive about them?

4. Can you be <u>objective</u> in an argument or debate or do you <u>take things personally</u>?

5. Do you enjoy playing <u>the devil's advocate</u>? What are some benefits to playing the devil's advocate?

6. What issues have you and your friends or family <u>agreed to disagree</u> on?

7. In what professions are good debating skills an <u>asset</u>?

8. Out of your friends, who is the most <u>argumentative?</u> Do you consider yourself an argumentative person? Explain.

9. Do you let people <u>have their say</u> in a debate or argument or do you tend to <u>cut them off</u>?

10. What are some <u>controversial</u> issues that are debated and discussed in your home country?

TAKE ME TO YOUR LEADER
Debate and Discussion along the campaign trail

Pre-Activity:

1. In small groups or with a partner, rate the following facilities and resources in this school on a scale from #1-#5, #1 being "GREAT", #5 being "TERRIBLE". Try to explain to each other why you feel the way you do.

____ COMPUTER ACCESS/QUALITY

____ HOMESTAY SUPPORT

____ BATHROOM FACILITIES

____ CONFLICT RESOLUTION

____ ACADEMIC SUPPORT

____ COMMUNICATION PRACTICE

____ EXTRACURRICULAR ACTIVITIES

____ TEXTBOOKS

____ FREE "GOODIES"

____ CLASSROOM COMFORT

____ MULTICULTURAL EXPERIENCE

____ AN ATTRACTIVE AND INTERESTING STUDENT BODY

2. As a class, discuss your answers and reasons for your rating choices. Write some brief notes next to the items above.

Function Practice

1. <u>Nominate</u> two or three (depending on the size of your class) "Candidates" from your class to run for "Student Body President". Once nominated, each candidate should also choose a "Campaign Manager", who will help them prepare for their campaign. The rest of the class should divide themselves into two groups.

2. If you are a Candidate or a Campaign Manager, look at "A". If you are in a group, look at "B".

GROUP A

1. If possible, the "Candidates" and their "Campaign Managers" should leave the classroom and find a private area to work. For 15-20 minutes, the "Candidates" and their "Campaign Managers" should choose 3 school problems (based on the Pre-activity) that they feel are very important and they promise to resolve. Each candidate must be able to explain why the issues are so important and how they are going to address them.

SCHOOL PROBLEM:	WHY IT'S IMPORTANT:	HOW TO SOLVE:
#1:		
#2:		
#3:		

1. "Candidates" and "Campaign Managers" will present their campaign platforms to 2 separate groups. "Candidates" should be prepared for questions about any school issue as well as the 3 they have chosen. "Candidates" will do most of the speaking, while "Campaign Managers" help with ideas. Use your "Debate and Discussion" expressions!

2. When "Candidates" have addressed both groups, the students will "vote"!

Homework:
   A. "Speaking" and "Journal" activities from The Homework Book
                              OR
   B. Ask a native speaker (homestay family/friend/another teacher) about the last time he/she voted and why he/she chose a particular candidate

GROUP B

1. Each group should choose 3 school problems that they think are very important and that should be resolved. Each group must be able to explain the problem, why it is so important, and suggestions for improvement to each candidate. Each student should write notes in the table below, so that they are prepared to speak.

SCHOOL PROBLEM:	WHY IT'S IMPORTANT:	SUGGESTIONS:
#1:		
#2:		
#3:		

2. When the "Candidates" return, they will address both groups in turns. Each group should respond to the "Candidates" ideas, but should also introduce the group's problems, reasons, and suggestions. Try to let everyone have a chance to speak and use your "Debate and Discussion" expressions!

3. When "Candidates" have addressed both groups, you should "vote" in a <u>secret ballot</u> for your "Student Body President" based on their promises and presentation!

<u>Homework:</u>
A. "Speaking" and "Journal" activities from <u>The Homework Book</u>
                       OR
B. Ask a native speaker (homestay family/friend/another teacher) about the last time he/she voted and why he/she chose a particular candidate

WE ARE ALL BUT ONE GRAIN OF SAND...
Debate and Discussion of Social Issues

#1_____

#2_____

#3_____

#4_____

#5_____

#6_____

Pre-Discussion:

In small groups or with a partner, discuss the social issues the pictures above reflect. Find out your partner's personal feelings and cultural perspective. Try to "name" each issue on the lines below each picture.

<u>Function Practice:</u>

1. In small groups or with a partner, discuss what debate-style questions could be connected to the pictures from <u>Pre-Discussion</u>.

> e.g.
> 1. Sometimes terrorism is the only way to get international attention for your cause
>   OR
> 2. The U.S. had no choice but to invade Afghanistan.

#1_____

_____

#2 _____

_____

#3_____

_____

#4_____

_____

#5_____

_____

#6_____

_____

2. As a class, share some of your "debate questions" and choose 2 you find the most interesting.

3. Your teacher will divide you into 4 groups and assign each group a debate question and a "PRO" or "CON" position REGARDLESS of your real position!

4. Spend 15-20 minutes with your group to organize your argument. Use facts, statistics, stories, descriptions etc… Your teacher will help you with ideas. You must also prepare to respond to your opponents' argument.

DEBATE POINTS:	EXAMPLES/EVIDENCE:
1.	
2.	
3.	
4.	

OPPONENTS' POSSIBLE ARGUMENTS:
1.
2.
3.

5. Join your opponents' group and begin your debate using your "Debate and Discussion" expressions. Your group and teacher will decide, based on your arguments and your use of the new expressions, which group "won" the debate!

Homework:
   A. "Speaking" and "Journal" activities from The Homework Book
                          OR
   B. Ask a native speaker (homestay family/friend/another teacher) how he/she feels about some of these issues.

TEACHER'S PAGES

Key:*

Initiating debate/discussion	Stating a position
Δ Why is/do __? ◊3 I can't believe that __ Δ2 How do you feel about __? ◊ It's unbelievable that __ Δ2 Do you have a position on__? Δ2 Where do you stand on__? Δ2 What's your take on__? Δ2 There's been a lot of controversy about__	◊3 I feel strongly that__ ◊5/O In my opinion, __ ◊3 I firmly believe that__ ◊ I think it's good/bad that__ ◊3 I've always thought that__ ◊5/O If you ask me, __ ◊3 I have to agree that__ ◊5/O Without a doubt, Δ Who can argue__? ◊5/O In my mind, ◊3 Everybody knows that__
Concession * ◊ It's true that__	**Disagreement** ◊3 I highly doubt that__
Rebuttal* Δ3/◊4/O Nonetheless, __ ◊ yet, it is also true that__ Δ3/◊4/O However, it doesn't change the fact that__ Δ3/◊4 although I still feel strongly that__ ◊2 but a more significant consideration is__ Δ3/◊3/◊4/O Nevertheless, I believe that__	**Summarizing and Concluding** ◊5/O In brief, ◊5/O In short, ◊5/O To sum up, ◊5/O Summing up, ◊2/O My point is__ ◊5/O In a nutshell, ◊5/O In conclusion, ◊5/O To wrap up, ◊2 The bottom line is__ ◊5/O When all is said and done, ◊2 My final point is __ ◊5 All in all,

Δ CHALLENGES:

Δ   Students sometimes struggle with rhetorical questions

Δ2   Students often neglect to use a gerund, noun phrase or clause following the preposition.

Δ3   Students confuse the meaning and structural differences between adverbial transitions and clauses.

◊ GRAMMAR EXPANSION:

◊   Practice with adjective complements

◊2   Practice with subject complements

◊3   Practice with noun clauses as objects

◊4   Practice with adverb clauses and adverbial transitions

◊5   Practice with connectors

O PRONUNCIATION:

O   Encourage students to take the natural pause that the comma represents

ALL   As always, remind students of the linking, syllable reduction, word and sentence stress, and intonation patterns of English.

*Order of gambits has been altered slightly

from *Function-all I: Intermediate Plus* by Fiona Bramble © Functionall Books 2006   www.eslenglish.ca

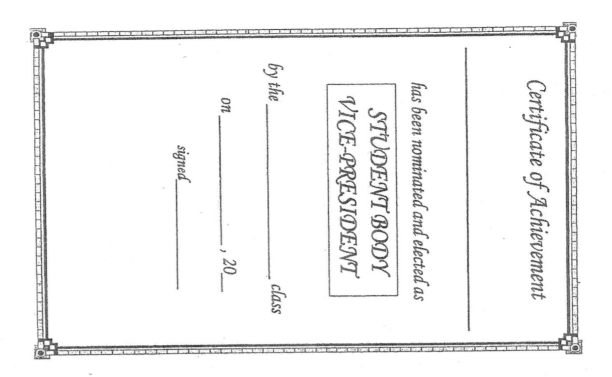

Certificate of Achievement

has been nominated and elected as

**STUDENT BODY
VICE-PRESIDENT**

by the _____ class

on _____ , 20 ___

signed _____

Certificate of Achievement

has been nominated and elected as

**STUDENT BODY
PRESIDENT**

by the _____ class

on _____ , 20 ___

signed _____

from *Function-all 1: Intermediate Plus* by Fiona Bramble © Functionall Books 2006   www.eslenglish.ca

TEACHER'S PAGES

Research websites for context2:

- www.behindthelabel.org (SWEATSHOPS)
- www.undp.org/teams/english/facts.htm (POVERTY)
- www.bambooweb.com/articles/g/a/gay_marriage.html (SAME SEX MARRIAGE)
- www.terrorismanswers.com/terrorism/introduction.html (TERRORISM)
- http://deathpenaltyinfo.msu.edu/ (CAPITAL PUNISHMENT)
- www.environment-agency.gov.uk (POLLUTION/ENVIRONMENT)
- www.amnesty.org AND www.greenpeace.org

Fact sheets for context2:

SWEATSHOPS	POVERTY
*There is currently no list of brand names that do not use sweatshops. *Apparel companies have brought many new jobs to all parts of the developing world *Most workers employed by sweatshops are not making anything near the sustainable wage rates or living wage for the country where they live and work. *In order to maintain jobs in manufacturing, workers must compete to see who will accept the lowest wages and the worst working conditions. *In the U.S., Canada, and Europe there are workers earning wages below the poverty line.	* Nearly 800 million people do not get enough food, 500 million of whom are chronically malnourished. *In industrial countries more than 100 million people live below the poverty line, more than 5 million people are homeless and 37 million are jobless *The net wealth of the 10 richest billionaires is $ 133 billion, more than 1.5 times the total national income of the least developed countries. *The proportion of human kind living in poverty has fallen faster in the past 50 years than in the previous 500 years. *Effective debt relief to the 20 poorest countries would cost $ 5.5 billion - equivalent to the cost of building EuroDisney.
SAME SEX MARRIAGE *Same-sex marriages are legal in only a few countries around the world. In Belgium and the Netherlands, it is fully legal. In Canada and the United States, the legality of same-sex marriage/civil union varies within each province or state. *Gay rights advocates assert marriage is a right which should not be limited to opposite-sex couples. *Opponents assert same-sex marriage cannot be allowed on moral and/or religious grounds, or on the grounds that it will lead to a breakdown of society.	**TERRORISM** *The point of terrorism is to use the psychological impact of violence or of the threat of violence to effect political change. *The religious terrorist often sees violence as an end in itself, as a divinely inspired way of serving a higher cause. *Al Qaeda represents the lunatic fringe of political thought in the Islamic world. *One flight departed the United States on September 20 [2001] with 26 passengers, most of them relatives of Osama Bin Ladin.
CAPITAL PUNISHMENT *Today, 66% of Americans support the death penalty. *78 countries use the death penalty. *During 2003, 1,146 prisoners were executed in 28 countries and 2,756 people were sentenced to death in 63 countries. *In 2003, 84 per cent of executions were in China, Iran, the USA and Viet Nam. *Scientific studies have consistently failed to find convincing evidence that the death penalty deters crime more effectively than other punishments.	**POLLUTION/ENVIRONMENT** *Meeting our energy demands currently requires the burning of fossil fuels (mainly) or generating nuclear energy. *The UK produces about 434 million tonnes of solid wastes per year but only reuses or recycles a fraction of this. *Rivers and lakes and seas support a range of fish species that help inform us about the quality of the environment and provide recreational activity for many people. *The EPA estimates 159 million Americans live in communities with unhealthy air.

TEACHER'S PAGES

Teaching Ideas:

1gambits
- ✓ elicit gambits from students prior to handing out gambit sheet; have a contest to see which team guesses the most from the list.
- ✓ in pairs or groups, make students responsible for suggesting expressions belonging to only one gambit aspect (e.g. "stating a position").

2warm-up
- ✓ this activity can be done 1) in small groups as instructed 2) as a class "mix and mingle" or 3) in pairs.
- ✓ another alternative is to stick a "POSITION CARD" to each student's back and have other students assert their opposition to the statement (without telling the student what his/her "POSITION CARD" states). The student can then guess what his/her "POSITION CARD" states and use his/her "CONCESSION CARD" or "DISAGREEMENT CARD" to respond to the other students' arguments.

3discussion
- ✓ pre-teach underlined vocabulary if necessary. Students can use drawing activities, charades, magazine scavenger hunts, etc... to guess or demonstrate meaning.
- ✓ cut questions into strips and a) post them around the class or school for a "run-read-ask" relay or b) put the strips in a bag or basket or c) do a "strip-exchange", in which students each have one question and, after asking one student, exchange questions with him/her and move on to another student. Repeat until everyone has heard and asked almost all questions.

context1
- ✓ this is meant to be light-hearted. It is important that the "loser" not feel like one. "Certificate" samples to be awarded can be found in the Teacher's Pages.
- ✓ encourage all students to participate. As in context2, students can be assigned specific gambit sections to ensure that they participate. For example, one student is responsible for "Initiating debate" and another for "Rebuttal". This will also help the students feel less overwhelmed!

context2
- ✓ pictures can be placed on an overhead or around the classroom for discussion
- ✓ the "Fact Sheets" in the Teacher's Pages can help generate ideas in each group. The "Fact Sheets" are far from comprehensive, they should only serve as springboards. An alternative would be to have students do some computer research beforehand. Some useful websites can be found in the Teacher's Pages.
- ✓ an oral presentation on a particular topic would be a good follow-up activity.

EXAGGERATION

1
I'm <u>so hungry that</u> I could eat a horse!!
This homework is <u>so easy that</u> I could do it with my eyes shut!

2
You <u>never</u> buy me anything!

He <u>always</u> gets the pretty girls!

3
<u>No one</u> loves me!

I don't understand <u>anything!</u>

4
It's <u>hotter than hell</u> in here!   She <u>knows more than Einstein</u>!

5
This is the <u>worst</u> day of my life!

My boyfriend is the <u>most thoughtful</u> guy in the world!

6
I've told you a <u>1000 times</u>!

It's <u>100 below</u> outside!

She lives <u>a million</u> miles away!

I don't have <u>a dime</u>!

7
You're going to <u>rip my arm off</u>!

I <u>can't breathe</u> in here!

My toes are <u>freezing</u>!

8
It <u>looks like a tornado hit your room</u>!   I feel <u>like I've been run over by a bus</u>!

1   "Exaggeration" using <u>so + adjective/adverb + that…</u>
2   "Exaggeration" using <u>adverbs of frequency (never, always, forever…)</u>
3   "Exaggeration" using <u>impersonal pronouns (everyone, no one, nothing…)</u>
4   "Exaggeration" using extreme <u>comparatives</u>
5   "Exaggeration" using extreme <u>superlatives</u>
6   "Exaggeration" using <u>#s for time, distance, money, temperature…</u>
7   "Exaggeration" using <u>extreme language and description</u>
8   "Exaggeration" <u>using simile with "as if" and "like"</u>

EXAGGERATION: TIC-TAC-TOE CARDS

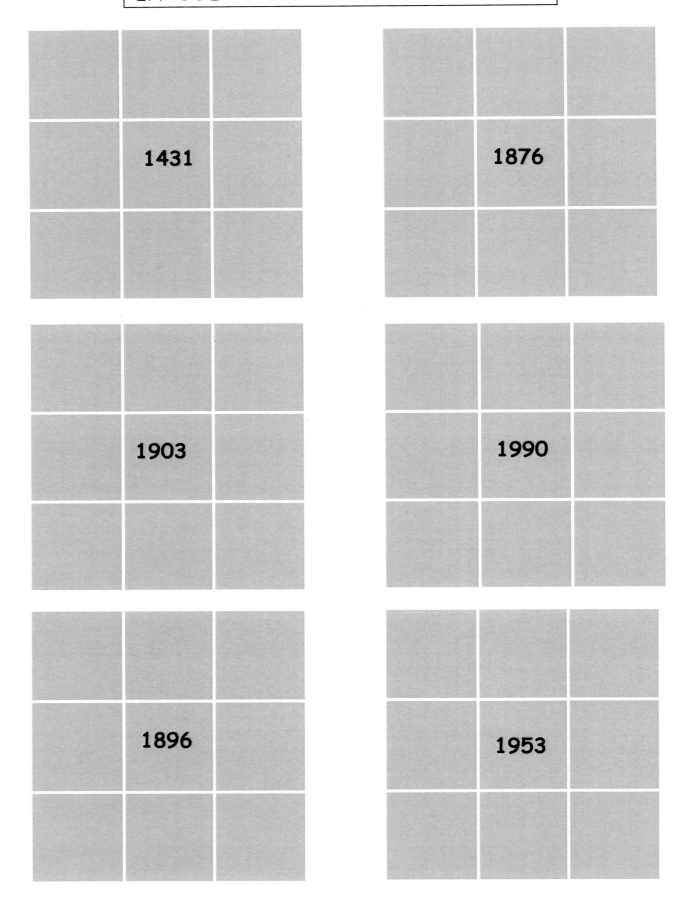

1431

1876

1903

1990

1896

1953

EXAGGERATION: STUDENT INSTRUCTIONS

1. Spend 5-10 minutes on your own to think of 4 important past dates in your life (a year, month, or specific date)
2. You and your partner should write your dates, one in each square, on your "TIC-TAC-TOE CARD"
3. Decide who will be "X" and who will be "O"
4. 'X" starts
5. "X" should choose a date that "O" wrote down
6. "O" should give clues, no more than 4, about that date, using the different types of "Exaggeration" SPEAKING ONLY!
7. "X" guesses what the date represents. If "X" guesses correctly, he or she can place and "x" on the square; if not, "O" places an "o" on the square
8. "O" then gets a turn and repeats steps 5-7, guessing "X"'s dates
9. Continue until all squares are filled or until there is a winner
10. Your teacher will give you a clue card for the center square; after reading the clues, "X" and "O" should write their answers down separately, without showing each other
11. When ready, your teacher will give you the correct answer; whoever is right (or closest) can place his/her "X" or "O"

1. Spend 5-10 minutes on your own to think of 4 important past dates in your life (a year, month, or specific date)
2. You and your partner should write your dates, one in each square, on your "TIC-TAC-TOE CARD"
3. Decide who will be "X" and who will be "O"
4. 'X" starts
5. "X" should choose a date that "O" wrote down
6. "O" should give clues, no more than 4, about that date, using the different types of "Exaggeration" SPEAKING ONLY!
7. "X" guesses what the date represents. If "X" guesses correctly, he or she can place and "x" on the square; if not, "O" places an "o" on the square
8. "O" then gets a turn and repeats steps 5-7, guessing "X"'s dates
9. Continue until all squares are filled or until there is a winner
10. Your teacher will give you a clue card for the center square; after reading the clues, "X" and "O" should write their answers down separately, without showing each other
11. When ready, your teacher will give you the correct answer; whoever is right (or closest) can place his/her "X" or "O"

from Function-all I: Intermediate Plus by Fiona Bramble © Functionall Books 2006   www.eslenglish.ca

EXAGGERATION: *DATE CLUE CARDS*

1431:
a. It was <u>hotter than hell</u>!
b. Charles VII <u>never even</u> tried!
c. She acted <u>as if she were guided by God.</u>
d. She was the <u>best French patriot ever</u>!

1876:
a. It sounded <u>like you were right next door</u>!
b. We could <u>never</u> live without it!
c. He's the <u>greatest Canadian</u>!
d. He worked on it <u>forever</u>!

1903:
a. <u>Everyone</u> thought they were crazy!
b. They were <u>higher than the clouds</u>!
c. It was over in <u>a second</u>!
d. They thought they'd <u>never</u> succeed!

1990:
a. It was <u>as if time had stood still</u>
b. Their currency was worth <u>nothing</u>!
c. People were <u>dying</u> to get to the other side!
d. Some people thought it wouldn't happen in <u>a million years</u>!

1896:
a. People came from <u>everywhere</u>!
b. Carl Schumann practically won <u>everything</u>!
c. Spyridon was <u>faster than the speed of light</u>!
d. James Connolly would have done <u>anything</u> to get there!

1953:
a. It was <u>colder than a penguin's nose</u>!
b. He felt <u>like he could touch the sky</u>!
c. It was <u>a death trap</u>!
d. It was <u>a million miles</u> high!

EXAGGERATION

"We exaggerate misfortune and happiness alike. We are never as bad off or as happy as we say we are"

Honore de Balzac, French Novelist (1799-1850)

<u>Discussion Questions</u>:
In pairs or small groups, discuss the following:

1. Do you agree with the quotation above? Does it suggest *why* people exaggerate?

2. To your partner, exaggerate how good or bad your life is using some of the methods you have learned.

3. Pronounce "exaggeration", then "exaggerate". Where is the stress in "exaggeration"? In "exaggerate"? What food item does the first syllable of both words sound like?

4. What is the difference between "exaggerate", "<u>embellish</u>" and "lie"?

5. Do you sometimes <u>blow something out of proportion</u> when you are angry or stressed? If so, why?

6. What kind of details would you add to a story to <u>spice it up</u>? Think about last weekend, what small embellishments would make it sound more interesting?

7. Do you have a friend or family member who you have to <u>take with a grain (or pinch) of salt</u>? Why?

8. Name some tales, legends, or myths that you think may have been exaggerated. Why do you think so? What might be some reasons for the exaggeration?

9. What excuses did you make to your parents that may have seemed a bit <u>farfetched</u> to them?

10. What do people exaggerate when they <u>brag</u>?

YO' MAMA
Using <u>exaggeration</u> to insult and brag

<u>Pre-discussion:</u>

In small groups or with a partner, compare these two statements:

> *"Yo' mama is so old that when she walked into an antique store, they kept her."*
>
> *"My mom is so beautiful, she should be a model"*

a. Which statement is an <u>insult</u>? A <u>boast</u>?
b. What do both statements have in common?
c. Would you say either statement? Why or why not?

<u>Function Practice:</u>

1.   With a partner, ORALLY complete the sentences below: EXAGGERATE!

Yo' mama is so crazy…
Yo' mama is so short…
Yo' mama is so loud…

My mom is so smart…
My mom is so stylish…
My mom is so sweet…

2.   Share your favorite answers with the class!

3.   For 5-10 minutes on your own, think of the qualities that you are proud of in connection with the people or things below:
    e.g.   <u>My parents</u>: My dad has a good position at work

    a. <u>My parents</u>:
    b. <u>My possessions</u>:
    c. <u>My talents</u>:
    d. <u>My school</u>:
    e. <u>My romantic life</u>:
    f. <u>My physical qualities</u>:
    g. <u>My country</u>:

4. With your partner, have a "bragging (or boasting) contest" about the people or things in step 3. Use as many as the different ways to exaggerate from your "Exaggeration" expressions as you can. Remember to use your <u>sentence stress!</u>

   e.g. **You**: My hair is soooooooooo shiny, you can see your reflection in it!
        Partner: Yeah? Well, my eyes are sexier than Angelina Jolie's!

5. For each topic, decide whose "boast" was better and write the winners' answers below:

      a. <u>My parents</u>:
         Winner:
         Answer:
      b. <u>My possessions</u>:
         Winner:
         Answer:
      c. <u>My talents</u>:
         Winner:
         Answer:
      d. <u>My school</u>:
         Winner:
         Answer:
      e. <u>My romantic life</u>:
         Winner:
         Answer:
      f. <u>My physical qualities</u>:
         Winner:
         Answer:
      g. <u>My country</u>:
         Winner:
         Answer:

6. Share your answers with another pair!

<u>Homework:</u>
   A. "Speaking" and "Journal" activities from <u>The Homework Book</u>
                   OR
   B. Ask a native speaker (homestay family/friend/another teacher) what he/she is <u>proud of</u> in his/her life. Listen to see if he/she uses any exaggeration!

THERE WAS THIS HUMONGOUS DOG IN THE WAY...
Using <u>Exaggeration</u> when making excuses

STUDENT A

<u>Introduction to Vocabulary:</u>

Below are some "extreme" words, expressions or idioms that are used in exaggeration and embellishment to make a story sound more interesting or convincing.

1. Do NOT show your partner your sheet!
2. Tell your partner the word or expression on the left. Ask your teacher if you need help with the pronunciation.
3. Your partner is allowed to ask ONLY Yes or No questions to try to guess the word or expression's "non-extreme" meaning
4. Give your partner a point for each correct (or close) guess

e.g,	You:	"costs a fortune"
	Partner:	Is it connected to money?
	You:	Yes
	Partner:	Is it "expensive"?
	You:	Yes! You got it!

WORD/EXPRESSION	MEANING
1. costs a fortune (verb phrase)	is expensive
2. suffocating (participle adjective)	stuffy/humid
3. at the crack of dawn (prepositional phrase)	early in the morning
4. humongous (adjective)	very large
5. to tower over someone (verb phr.)	to be tall
6. a pigsty (noun)	a messy area

5. Ask your partner to tell you his/her words or expressions and ask YES or NO questions to guess the meaning.

WORD/EXPRESSION	MEANING
1.	
2.	
3.	
4.	
5.	
6.	

THERE WAS THIS HUMONGOUS DOG IN THE WAY...
Using <u>Exaggeration</u> when making excuses

STUDENT B

Introduction to Vocabulary:

Below are some "extreme" words, expressions or idioms that are used in exaggeration and embellishment to make a story sound more interesting or convincing.

1. Do NOT show your partner your sheet!
2. Tell your partner the word or expression on the left. Ask your teacher if you need help with the pronunciation.
3. Your partner is allowed to ask ONLY Yes or No questions to try to guess the word or expression's "non-extreme" meaning
4. Give your partner a point for each correct (or close) guess

> e.g, You: "filthy"
> Partner: Is it a noun?
> You: No
> Partner: Is it an "adjective"?
> You: Yes
> Partner: Does it describe people?
> You: Yes

WORD/EXPRESSION	MEANING
1. filthy (adjective)	very dirty
2. hammered (adjective)	very drunk
3. packed (adjective)	very busy
4. (a) kajillion (adjective)	a large number
5. kill (verb)	hurt
6. cuts off one's circulation (vb. phr.)	is too tight

5. Ask your partner to tell you his/her words or expressions and ask YES or NO questions to guess the meaning.

WORD/EXPRESSION	MEANING
1.	
2.	
3.	
4.	
5.	
6.	

<u>Function Practice:</u>

1. **With your partner, read the "excuse" below and try to change the <u>underlined</u> words into more "extreme" synonyms from the "Introduction to Vocabulary". Which version is a more convincing excuse?**

   Question: Why are you so late for class?

   Excuse: Well, it's a long story, but I had to make my own lunch for the <u>second</u> time this week and my host mother's kitchen was <u>messy</u>, so I had to clean it up before I could make my lunch. I think my host father was <u>drunk</u> last night because he was singing in the kitchen <u>early in the morning</u> and there were beer bottles on the counter. Anyway, I wanted to have a shower, but my host father was in the bathroom and said he couldn't come out because his head and stomach were <u>hurting</u>, so I had to wait <u>a few</u> minutes.
   As I was getting dressed, I realized my shirt was <u>very dirty</u> and my jeans were <u>too tight</u>, so I had to find something else to wear. By the time I got to the bus stop, there was a <u>big</u> line and when the bus arrived it was already <u>full</u>. I could have taken a taxi, but they are <u>expensive</u>, so I had to walk to school. Sorry teacher!

3. **Complete the questions below and ask each other what reasons you each have for your actions. They do not have to be real situations. Use your new vocabulary and your "Exaggeration" expressions!**

   a. Why didn't you…?
   b. Where were you…?
   c. How could you…?
   d. Why are you…?

4. **As a class, share your favorite excuses!**

<u>Homework:</u>

A. **"Speaking" and "Journal" activities from <u>The Homework Book</u>**
                            OR

B. **Choose 6 of the new words from "Introduction to Vocabulary" and ask a native speaker (homestay family/friend/another teacher) what people or places the words make him/her think of.**
   e.g. A: Does anyone "tower over you"?
           B: My father-in-law is pretty tall.

TEACHER'S PAGES

Key:

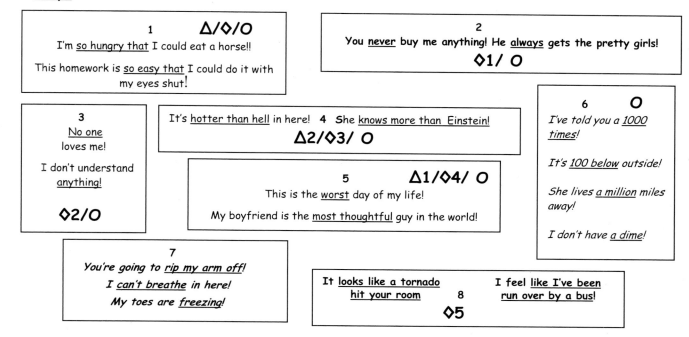

1   Δ/◊/O
I'm <u>so hungry that</u> I could eat a horse!!

This homework is <u>so easy that</u> I could do it with my eyes shut!

2
You <u>never</u> buy me anything! He <u>always</u> gets the pretty girls!
◊1/ O

3
<u>No one</u> loves me!

I don't understand <u>anything</u>!

◊2/O

It's <u>hotter than hell</u> in here! **4** She <u>knows more than</u> Einstein!
Δ2/◊3/ O

5   Δ1/◊4/ O
This is the <u>worst</u> day of my life!
My boyfriend is the <u>most thoughtful</u> guy in the world!

6   O
I've told you a <u>1000 times</u>!

It's <u>100 below</u> outside!

She lives <u>a million</u> miles away!

I don't have <u>a dime</u>!

7
You're going to <u>rip my arm off</u>!
I <u>can't breathe</u> in here!
My toes are <u>freezing</u>!

It <u>looks like a tornado hit your room</u>   **8**   I feel <u>like I've been run over by a bus</u>!
◊5

Δ CHALLENGES:

Δ   Students struggle with the "unreal" aspect of hyperbole and the use of modals, especially "could". Students may instead use the "real' aspect, e.g. I was so hungry that I ate a whole pizza (which may or may not result in exaggeration)

Δ1   Students struggle with the syllable rules for superlative constructions

Δ2   Students struggle with the syllable rules for comparative constructions

◊ GRAMMAR EXPANSION:

◊   Practice with <u>so...that and such...that</u> *Note the use of <u>hyperbole</u>

◊1   Practice with <u>adverbs of frequency</u>

◊2   Practice with <u>impersonal pronouns</u>

◊3   Practice with <u>comparatives</u> *Note the use of "extreme" comparatives *Can also be used in a conditional structure for exaggeration, e.g. If you were going any slower, you'd be going backwards

◊4   Practice with <u>superlatives</u> *Note use of "extreme" prepositional phrases, e.g. "in the whole world", "of my life", "on earth" etc...

◊5   Practice with <u>like</u> and <u>as if</u> in similes

O PRONUNCIATION:

O   The underlined elements, for the most part, should be stressed, as stress is a major aspect of exaggeration, e.g. You NEVER buy me ANYTHING! (adverb and pronoun)

ALL   As always, remind students of the linking, syllable reduction, sentence stress, and intonation patterns of English.

TEACHER'S PAGES

Teaching Ideas:

1gambits

- ✓ introduce function by talking about your weekend, previous night etc...Ask students what they notice about your story or the way you told it
- ✓ because these gambits lend themselves to independent grammar structures, perhaps only introduce two or three at a time before giving students the sheet

2warm-up

- ✓ the concept is a little confusing, so student copies of the instructions can be handy for reference
- ✓ this is intended to act as a springboard for the function, so limiting the clues to 4 per time period keeps things moving
- ✓ perhaps do one "game" on an overhead with your own dates to give an example and get things started or simply have students use their own dates on blank tic-tac-toe cards!
- ✓ ANSWERS:

DATE	EVENT
1431	year Joan of Arc was burned at the stake
1876	year the telephone was invented by Alexander G. Bell
1903	year of the Wright Bros. first flight
1990	year the Berlin Wall came down
1896	year of the first modern Olympics
1953	year Sir Edmund Hillary reached the summit of Everest

3discussion

- ✓ pre-teach underlined vocabulary if necessary. Students can use drawing activities, charades, magazine scavenger hunts, etc... to guess or demonstrate meaning
- ✓ cut questions into strips and a) post them around the class or school for a "run-read-ask" relay or b) put the strips in a bag or basket or c) do a "strip-exchange", in which students each have one question and, after asking one student, exchange questions with him/her and move on to another student. Repeat until everyone has heard and asked almost all questions d) organize students into two "speaking lines" facing each other. Have one line continuously move down after two facing students have asked each other their questions

from *Function-all I: Intermediate Plus* by Fiona Bramble © Functionall Books 2006   www.eslenglish.ca

TEACHER'S PAGES

context1

✓ there are a number of "Yo' Mama" joke websites for practice
e.g. http://members.tripod.com/donaldchase/jokes/yomamma.htm
✓ one website for so...that exaggeration practice is:
http://www.better-english.com/grammar/sothat.htm
✓ again, beware of the use of hyperbole with so...that
✓ sentence stress is very important in Exaggeration

> **Note:** There may be some strong cultural resistance to the "yo mama" concept. Perhaps explain to students that they are considered ritual insults in urban street culture, particularly among African-Americans. Some historians also contend that "mama" was actually code for "master" and that slaves were insulting each other's masters, not mothers!

context2

✓ the "Introduction to Vocabulary" can be done in teams as a class
✓ ANSWERS for "Function Practice"

Non-exaggerated version

Well, it's a long story, but I had to make my own lunch for the <u>second</u> time this week and my host mother's kitchen was <u>messy</u>, so I had to clean it up before I could make my lunch. I think my host father was <u>drunk</u> last night because he was in singing in the kitchen <u>early in the morning</u> and there were beer bottles on the counter. Anyway, I wanted to have a shower, but my host father was in the bathroom and said he couldn't come out because his head and stomach were <u>hurting</u>, so I had to wait <u>a few</u> minutes. As I was getting dressed, I realized my shirt was <u>very dirty</u> and my jeans were <u>too tight</u>, so I had to find something else to wear. By the time I got to the bus stop, there was a <u>big</u> line and when the bus arrived it was already <u>busy</u>. I could have taken a taxi, but they are <u>expensive</u>, so I had to walk to school. Sorry teacher!

Exaggerated version

Well, it's a long story, but I had to make my own lunch for the <u>kajillionth</u> time this week and my host mother's kitchen was <u>a pigsty</u>, so I had to clean it up before I could make my lunch. I think my host father was <u>hammered</u> last night because he was in singing in the kitchen <u>at the crack of dawn</u> and there were beer bottles on the counter. Anyway, I wanted to have a shower, but my host father was in the bathroom and said he couldn't come out because his head and stomach were <u>killing (him)</u>, so I had to wait <u>a kajillion</u> minutes. As I was getting dressed, I realized my shirt was <u>filthy</u> and my jeans were <u>cutting off my circulation</u>, so I had to find something else to wear. By the time I got to the bus stop, there was a <u>humongous</u> line and when the bus arrived it was already <u>packed</u>. I could have taken a taxi, but they <u>cost a fortune</u>, so I had to walk to school. Sorry teacher!

Guessing

99% CERTAIN
I'm sure/certain that___
There's no question that___
It's impossible that___
Fat chance that___
There's no way in hell that___
For sure,
*(It) can't/couldn't (have)___
I have no doubt that___
I'd swear/could have sworn___

80-98% CERTAIN →
*(It) probably___
In all likelihood,
It's very likely that___
I'd bet that___
I wouldn't bet on ___
I'm fairly certain that___
There's a strong possibility___
There's a good chance that___
I'm almost certain that___
*(It) must (not)(have)___
*(It) has to ___/has got to ___
*(It) should (not)(have)___
I have a sneaking suspicion that___

50% CERTAIN
It's possible that___
There's every chance that___
Perhaps,
Maybe,
Possibly,
I wouldn't be surprised if___
It's easy to believe that___
*(It) may/might (not)(have)___
*(It) could (have) ___

LESS THAN 50% CERTAIN →
There's a slight chance that___
If___, then maybe___
There's a remote possibility that___
You never know
Anything's possible
Just maaaaaaaayyyyyybe___
It's doubtful that___

*the words in parentheses [( )] can be substituted or omitted

GUESSING: MUGSHOTS
STUDENT A

1

2

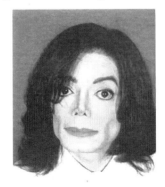

3

4

Santa Barbara County Sheriff's Dept.

11/20/2003
Photo Image of:
NAME: JACKSON, MICHAEL
RAC: B   SEX: M
DOB: 8/29/1958 AGE: 45
HGT: 511   WGT: 120
BLD: CMP:
HAI: BLK   EYE: BRO
MKS:
BOOKING #: 621785

5

GUESSING: MUGSHOTS

STUDENT B

6

7

8

9

10

from *Function-all 1: Intermediate Plus* by Fiona Bramble © Functionall Books 2006   www.eslenglish.ca

GUESSING: MUGSHOTS

GUESS CARDS

I'm sure that it's <u>name of person in picture</u> because <u>reason</u>
I'd bet that he <u>crime he committed</u> because <u>reason</u>
It's probably <u>name of person in picture</u> because <u>reason</u>
I wouldn't be surprised if he <u>crime he committed</u> because <u>reason</u>
Just maaaaaaayyybe he <u>crime he committed</u> because <u>reason</u>
It's very likely that he <u>crime he committed</u> because <u>reason</u>

I have no doubt that it's <u>name of person in picture</u> because <u>reason</u>
In all likelihood, he <u>crime he committed</u> because <u>reason</u>
There's a strong possibility that it's <u>name of person in picture</u> because <u>reason</u>
Maybe he <u>crime he committed</u> because <u>reason</u>
He can't have <u>crime he committed</u> because <u>reason</u>
I wouldn't bet on him having <u>crime he committed</u> because <u>reason</u>

There's no question that it's <u>name of person in picture</u> because <u>reason</u>
Fat chance that he did/didn't <u>crime he committed</u> because <u>reason</u>
I'm almost certain that it's <u>name of person in picture</u> because <u>reason</u>
He must have <u>crime he committed</u> because <u>reason</u>
Perhaps he <u>crime he committed</u> because <u>reason</u>
It's impossible that he <u>crime he committed</u> because <u>reason</u>

For sure, it's <u>name of person in picture</u> because <u>reason</u>
There's every chance that he <u>crime he committed</u> because <u>reason</u>
It could be <u>name of person in picture</u> because <u>reason</u>
I have a sneaking suspicion that he <u>crime he committed</u> because <u>reason</u>
There's a slight chance he <u>crime he committed</u> because <u>reason</u>
Possibly, he <u>crime he committed</u> because <u>reason</u>

It's got to be <u>name of person in picture</u> because <u>reason</u>
There's no way in hell he did/didn't <u>crime he committed</u> because <u>reason</u>
It's possible that it's <u>the name of person in picture</u> because <u>reason</u>
It's easy to believe that <u>crime he committed</u> because <u>reason</u>
There's a remote possibility that he <u>crime he committed</u> because <u>reason</u>
He may not have <u>crime he committed</u> because <u>reason</u>

GUESSING

"The more I see, the less I know for sure"

John Lennon, Writer-Musician (1940-1980)

Discussion Questions:

In pairs or small groups, discuss the following:

1. What do you think John Lennon meant in the quotation above? What John Lennon or Beatles song do you know? Hum or sing it to your partner!

2. Do you think we become more, or less certain about things as we age? Explain. What is something you were absolutely certain about when you were younger that you are less sure about now?

3. Why do we guess? To make conversation? To get closer to an answer?

4. What is an "intelligent guess"? Do you think you make intelligent guesses? Explain.

5. How old is your teacher? Take a wild guess! What is a "wild guess"?

6. What are some universal mysteries that people can't stop speculating about?

7. When you have a hunch about something, do you ignore it or follow your gut? Why?

8. Do you need proof of something before you form an opinion? Why or why not?

9. Do people assume things about you that aren't true? Why do they assume these things? "To assume makes an ASS out of U and ME" What does this expression mean?

10. Tell your partner 2 things you are 99% certain about and 2 things you are less than 50% certain about and explain why.

from *Function-all 1: Intermediate Plus* by Fiona Bramble © Functionall Books 2006 www.eslenglish.ca

I WONDER HOW I GOT THIS WEIRD RASH?
Guessing about our bodies

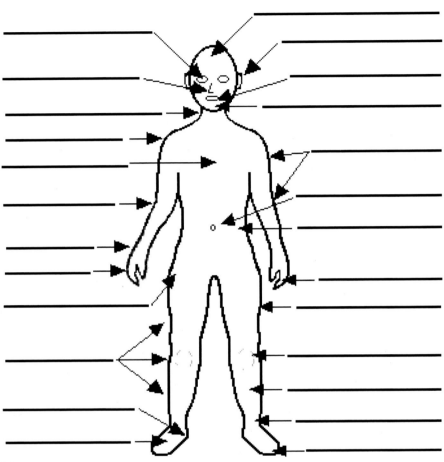

Pre-activity:

1.   In small groups or with a partner, label the body parts above using the vocabulary below:
      *there are some extra words; try to place them correctly!

forehead	thigh	neck	*calf
ear	knee/kneecap	shoulder	heel
mouth	shin	chest/breast	belly button
chin	ankle	wrist	waist
upper arm	toes	fingers	*armpit
elbow	eye/eyelid	hip	*earlobe
hand	nose	leg	*forearm
*nape	*sole	*eyebrow	*bridge
*butt/bum	*crotch	*pinky	foot

2. **With your partner, guess where on the body one can get:**

a. a rash   c. a pimple   e. a cramp   g. a hickey

b. a blister   d. a bruise   f. indigestion   h. a spare tire

3. **With your partner, guess what area on the body can be:**

a. swollen   c. itchy   e. sprained   g. broken

b. stuffed up   d. sweaty   f. pale   h. sore

4. **Share your answers as a class.**

Function Practice:

People often GUESS what is happening to their bodies and to others' bodies, for example:

A: I wonder how I got this **bruise** on my **bum**?

B: You <u>must have</u> bumped into something.

A: Yeah, I think <u>I might have hit</u> it on the desk when I came in this morning.

B: That's <u>probably</u> it.

1. Like the example above, tell your partner about anything that is happening or has happened to *your* body and GUESS the reasons why you are having or have had that problem (even if you already know why). Use your "Guessing" expressions! If you really don't have anything strange happening, make it up or talk about someone else!

2. You can reply to each other's GUESSES with:

Yeah, that's it!
Maybe
I doubt it
No way

Homework:

A. "Speaking" and "Journal" activities from <u>The Homework Book</u>
OR

B. Talk to a native speaker (homestay family/friend/another teacher) about a "body mystery" you have. Listen for the GUESSES he/she makes about the cause of your problem.

EATING TACOS AND HUNTING CROCODILES
<u>Guessing</u> about stereotypes

Pre-discussion:

In small groups or with a partner, discuss the following:

1. What is a *stereotype*?
2. Are stereotypes true? False? Bad? Good?
3. Do you sometimes stereotype people?
4. Why do we stereotype?
5. What are some common stereotypes connected to the following:
   a. gender
   b. professions
   c. cultures
   d. age groups
   e. regions (e.g. city/countryside)

Function Practice:

1. **With your partner, make a list of the different cultures represented by you, your classmates, and your teacher:**

CULTURE	STEREOTYPES
#1	a. b. c.
#2	a. b. c.
#3	a. b. c.
#4	a. b. c.
#5	a. b. c.

2. **Using your "Guessing" expressions, discuss and list some stereotypes (true or false!) that are common to each culture, including your own.**

    e.g. <u>Fat chance</u> that you can be warm in Canada.

    OR

    <u>There's a good chance</u> you'll get robbed in New York

3. On your own or with your partner, ask your other classmates and teacher about the stereotypes of their cultures. Use your "Guessing" expressions to give a *reason* for your belief

e.g. <u>I'd bet</u> that Mexicans eat tacos everyday because Taco Time is their favorite fast food place!

OR

I <u>wouldn't be surprised</u> if all Saudis hated westerners because of the problems in the Middle East.

To reply to statements about your own culture, you can say:

That's actually true.
In the past, but not now.
Some people do but not everybody.
That's really uncommon.
That's b.s.!
That's not true at all!

4. After you have spoken to someone from every culture, talk to your partner about what you found out and write some of the stereotypes from step 1 in the columns below:

TRUE	PARTIALLY TRUE	NOT TRUE
1.	1.	1.
2.	2.	2.

5. If there is time, share some of your answers as a class!

<u>Homework</u>:
A.   "Speaking" and "Journal" activities from <u>The Homework Book</u>
OR
B.   Talk to a native speaker (homestay family/friend/another teacher) about the stereotypes he/she had of your culture in the past and make some guesses about his/her culture.

TEACHER'S PAGES

Key:

```
                                    99% CERTAIN
        ←
        ◇         I'm sure/certain that__
        ◇1        There's no question that__
        ◇         It's impossible that__
        ◇1        Fat chance that__
        ◇1        There's no way in hell that__
        Δ1/◇2/O   *(It) can't/couldn't (have)__
        ◇1        I have no doubt that__
        Δ1/O  I'd swear/could have sworn that__
```

```
                    80-98% CERTAIN          →
        Δ         I wouldn't bet on __
        ◇         I'm fairly certain that__
        ◇1        There's a strong possibility__
        ◇1        There's a good chance that__
        ◇         I'm almost certain that__
        Δ1/◇2/O      *(It) must (not)(have )__
        Δ1/◇2/O      *(It) has to __/has got to __
        Δ1/◇2/O      *(It) should (not)(have)__
        ◇1        I have a sneaking suspicion that__
```

```
                                    50% CERTAIN
        ←
        ◇         It's possible that__
        ◇1        There's every chance that__
        ◇         It's easy to believe that__
        Δ1/◇2/O  *(It) may/might not)(have)__
        Δ1 /◇2/O *(It) could (have) __
```

```
                LESS THAN 50% CERTAIN     →
        ◇1        There's a slight chance that__
        ◇1        There's a remote possibility that__
        ◇         It's doubtful that__
```

Δ CHALLENGES:

Δ   Students struggle with the gerund phrase that usually follows the preposition, especially the use of an object pronoun vs. a possessive adjective, e.g. I wouldn't bet on <u>his/him</u> being there tonight.

Δ1   Students struggle with many aspects of modals and modal perfects
  - ➢ 'must' and 'have to': necessity vs. guessing (or inference)
  - ➢ 'should': advice vs. expectation
  - ➢ 'can't/couldn't' (99% certainty) vs. 'could' (50% certainty)
  - ➢ usage of 'has to' and 'have to': has to →has got to→ got to (/gɔːdə/)
  - ➢ modals vs. modal perfects
  - ➢ 'could have sworn' is a unique expression

◇ GRAMMAR EXPANSION:

◇   Practice with noun clauses as adjective complements

◇1   Practice with noun clauses as noun complements

◇2   Practice with modals and modal perfects

O PRONUNCIATION:

O   Students neglect the reduction in the modal perfect form, e.g. He must have /mʌstə/ or /mʌstəv/ been bitten by a bug.

ALL   Sentence stress often falls on the "word of certainty", e.g. It's POSSIBLE that he was bitten by a bug.

Mugshot Answers for Warm-up:

NAME	DETAILS
1: Keanu Reeves Actor (The Matrix)	The police arrested Keanu Reeves in 1993 for drunk driving. He had been driving very carelessly. Keanu was released after his confession.
NAME	**DETAILS**
2: Marilyn Manson Singer/Musician	Arrested in 2001, for sexual assault on a security guard. Paid a $4000 fine.
NAME	**DETAILS**
3: Tim Allen Actor (The Santa Clause)	Allen spent 28 months in jail after being arrested for attempted drug-dealing in 1978.
NAME	**DETAILS**
4: Elvis Presley Singer/Musician	The photo was taken in 1970 at the FBI headquarters in Washington DC. Elvis collected guns and badges. He had the mugshots taken when he went to visit Nixon to get a DEA badge for his collection.
NAME	**DETAILS**
5: Michael Jackson Singer	In November, 2003, arrested on child molestation charges. Bail was set at $3 million.
NAME	**DETAILS**
6: Hugh Grant Actor (About a Boy)	Charged with indecent appearance. Los Angeles police noticed a girl, suspected to be a prostitute, stepping into a '95 BMW, the driver of which was Hugh Grant.
NAME	**DETAILS**
7: Al Pacino Actor (Godfather/Ocean's Eleven)	Charged with carrying a concealed weapon in 1961. The police searched the car and found a 38 caliber pistol. Pacino couldn't pay the $2000 bail, so Pacino ended up spending three days in jail.
NAME	**DETAILS**
8: Bill Gates Entrepreneur (Microsoft)	On April 29th, 1975, at the age of 19, Gates was arrested by the Albuquerque Police department. The charges were speeding and driving without a license.
NAME	**DETAILS**
9: Frank Sinatra Singer/Performer	In 1938, a 23-year-old Sinatra was arrested on charges of seduction and adultery - charges were later dismissed in New Jersey.
NAME	**DETAILS**
10: Christian Slater Actor (Broken Arrow/Alone in the Dark)	Charged with carrying a loaded gun without a license in his luggage at J.F.K International airport in 1994, when his luggage activated the security alarm. In his bag was a 7.65-caliber Baretta, which he didn't have a license for. Slater was sentenced to three days of social service at a children's safe house.

TEACHER'S PAGES

Teaching Ideas:

1 gambits
- ✓ elicit gambits from students prior to handing out gambit sheet; have a contest to see which team guesses the most from the list.
- ✓ in pairs or groups, make students responsible for suggesting expressions belonging to only one gambit aspect (e.g. "99% CERTAIN")
- ✓ have students organize gambits into formal or informal columns

2 warm-up
- ✓ each student in a pair can have his own "photo sheet" (with or without answers) or photos can be put on a overhead or placed around the room
- ✓ each "guess card" is different and can be assigned to a student for controlled practice, or to a picture for more varied gambit practice.
- ✓ mugshot descriptions can be found in the Teacher's Pages

3 discussion
- ✓ cut questions into strips and a) post them around the class or school for a "run-read-ask" relay or b) put the strips in a bag or basket or c) do a "strip-exchange", in which students each have one question and, after asking one student, exchange questions with him/her and move on to another student. Repeat until everyone has heard and asked most questions.

context 1
- ✓ "body diagram" can be played as a game of "Simon Says" (e.g. Simon says: touch your bum) OR pairs can stick vocabulary post-its on their partners' matching bits OR a version of the game of "Twister" (e.g. put your armpit on the red circle) OR the diagram can be enlarged for the wall and teams have a colour-coded vocabulary relay race to place the vocabulary in the right spot!
- ✓ this context is vocabulary heavy, so depending on the level, you might want to leave the Pre-Activity #2, 3, and 4 for review of body parts the next day and THEN start the Function Practice
- ✓ if students are slow to speak or truly have no body issues to talk about, consider bringing in, or having as back up, pictures of people with weird stuff on them (medical books and journals are a good source; dermatology websites are great too:
  e.g. http://www.lib.uiowa.edu/hardin/md/dermpictures.html

context 2
- ✓ bring in pictures/movies which exhibit stereotyped images to introduce concept
- ✓ be conscious of cultural sensitivies, but explore them!

from *Function-all 1: Intermediate Plus* by Fiona Bramble © Functionall Books 2006 www.eslenglish.ca

ASKING ABOUT LIKES AND DISLIKES

What do you think about/of_____?
Do you like_____?
Have you ever had/tried/seen_____?

EXPRESSING LIKES AND DISLIKES

I am crazy about_

I can't do without_

I love__

I really like__

I can't get enough of__

__is my favorite__

__is awesome

__rocks

__turns me on

__is just my thing

__is right up my alley

__is sweet

I don't mind__

__is o.k.

__is not bad

__is alright/all right

__is fine

__will do

__is better than a kick in the pants

I despise__

I loathe__

I hate__

I can't stand__

I dislike__

__is my least favorite__

__turns me off

__is not my cup of tea

I'm not crazy about__

I don't care for__

I can live without__

__is lame

__sucks

LIKES AND DISLIKES: *FIND SOMEONE WHO/WHOSE... BINGO*

<u>is crazy about</u> snowboarding	**DOESN'T MIND CLEANING THE TOILET**	*LOATHES CIGARETTE SMOKE*	thinks Celine Dion is <u>lame</u>	**<u>can live without</u> chocolate**
<u>can't stand</u> getting spam	wardrobe <u>sucks</u>	English class <u>makes</u> his/her day	*<u>despises</u> an ex-boy/girlfriend*	**THINKS JOHNNY DEPP IS <u>AWESOME</u>**
JOB <u>IS RIGHT UP HIS/HER ALLEY</u>	dislikes apologizing to people	*F R E E*	<u>ISN'T CRAZY ABOUT</u> GETTING UP EARLY	can't do <u>without</u> his/her car
*is **<u>turned off</u>** by mustaches*	**THINKS OCTOPUS <u>ISN'T BAD</u>**	*LOVES CUDDLING*	thinks grammar <u>is all right</u>	<u>can't get enough of</u> Starbucks' Lattes.
thinks his/her hostmother or hostfather's cooking <u>is better than a kick in the pants</u>	**<u>hates</u> the way some people pronounce his/her name**	*got a recent birthday present that was <u>not</u> his/her cup of tea*	admits that intelligence really <u>turns</u> him/her on	really likes being tickled

LIKES AND DISLIKES

"To like and dislike the same things, that is indeed true friendship."

Sallust, *The War with Catiline*, *Roman historian & politician (86 BC - 34 BC)*

Discussion Questions:
In pairs or small groups, discuss the following:

1. Do you agree with the quotation above? Why or why not? Do you and your closest friends share the same likes and dislikes?

2. Have you ever <u>faked</u> liking or disliking something (for example, drinking, or the opera) so that you could <u>fit in</u> with a group?

3. Have you ever had something that you previously disliked <u>grow on you</u>?

4. Which foods did you <u>despise</u> as a child that you like now? What changed?

5. Are you <u>fickle</u> with the things you like and don't like? Explain.

6. Do you think our "likes and dislikes" are partly <u>cultural</u>? If so, what do you think most people from your country would NOT like about the country you are in now? What are some cultural differences?

7. Show your partner your facial expression when you really don't like something!

8. Are you <u>open-minded</u> about changing your likes and dislikes?

9. Name one thing you love about yourself and one thing you <u>can't stand.</u>

10. Do you think it is important to sometimes do things we don't like? Why or why not?

FRESHLY BAKED BREAD AND GYM SOCKS
Smells we like and dislike

Freshly cut grass   *ARMPITS*   **ORANGES**

Burning rubber   barbecued meat   LIBRARIES

freshly ground coffee   *lavender*   chlorine

gas   the ocean   LINE-DRIED SHEETS

CIGARS   *lilies*   PAINT

burning leaves   WET DOG   *summer rain*

Pre-discussion:
In small groups or with a partner, discuss the following:

1. Can you connect any of the smells above to your past? Is it a good memory or a bad memory?
    You can start your sentence with: _____(smell)_____ reminds me of the time _____(memory)_____.
2. Which of the above smells is the most <u>sentimental</u> for you? The most relaxing? The most <u>stimulating</u>? The strongest?
3. How are the smells in this country different from those in your home country?
4. Do you have <u>a sensitive nose</u>?
5. What does your partner smell like? ☺

Function Practice:

1. **With a partner, use "Expressing Likes and Dislikes" to *orally* describe how you feel about the smells above and any other smells you like or dislike. Explain why and use many *different* expressions!**

    e.g. <u>I am crazy about</u> line-dried sheets because they smell so fresh and remind me of spring!

2. **Report your partner's likes and dislikes to a new partner and vice versa. Record what your new partner tells you below.**

    e.g. Yoo Lim <u>loathes</u> the smell of raw chicken but thinks armpit smells are <u>awesome</u>! She <u>doesn't mind</u> cigars.

armpits	cigars	raw chicken

Classmate's name _____

3. **Your teacher will ask everyone to report the results as a group. Try to remember some of the expressions that your partners used. Don't look at your "Expressing Likes and Dislikes" sheet!**

Homework:

  A.   "Speaking" and "Journal" activities from <u>The Homework Book</u>
                                  OR

  B.   Ask a native speaker (homestay family/friend/another teacher) some of the questions from "Pre-Discussion".

OPPOSITES ATTRACT...?
Personalities we like and dislike

Introduction to Vocabulary:

Match the following words to the type of person they describe:

RESERVED

SHY

LAZY

IMPULSIVE

FICKLE

SHALLOW

STUCK UP

TRENDY

SENSITIVE

CONSERVATIVE

A person who is quiet and feels uncomfortable around strangers

A person who thinks he/she is in "a higher class" than others

A person who follows traditional styles and social customs.

A person who doesn't like to work hard, emotionally or physically

A person who is quiet and doesn't easily share his/her feelings

A person who does things without thinking much about them first

A person who follows the most current styles

A person for whom material things and appearance are most important

A person who changes his/her mind often about what he/she likes.

A person who understands other people's feelings

Function Practice:

1. With a partner, use "Expressing Likes and Dislikes" to *orally* describe what types of people you like and dislike and *why*. Use many different expressions and some of the new vocabulary.

   e.g. I <u>can't stand</u> people who are shallow because I can't really trust that they like me for who I am, not what I look like.

2. From the photos and descriptions below, choose a new friend or date for your partner based on what he/she has told you about his/her likes and dislikes:

I <u>don't mind</u> going out but I <u>love</u> spending time at the beach or at home in front of the fire. <u>I'm not really crazy</u> about sports but cycling <u>is o.k.</u> I <u>like</u> to think about things for a while before I make any decisions.

I <u>can definitely live without</u> going to school and homework <u>is lame</u> for sure! <u>I'm crazy about</u> the Simpsons and <u>can't get enough of</u> reality t.v. *Extreme Makeover is* <u>awesome</u>!

Going out to the club on the weekends is <u>right up my alley</u>. Intense people are definitely <u>not my cup of tea.</u> I also <u>love</u> to shop but sometimes I spend way too much.

I <u>despise</u> trendy people and snobs and think consumerism <u>sucks</u>. I <u>don't care for</u> people who spill their guts all the time either. I <u>can't stand</u> being stuck in one place and get bored fast!

I <u>can't do without</u> my family and friends and I think it's important to treat your elders with respect. I <u>loathe</u> having to go to parties because I don't know what to say and drunk people act a little stupid.

Strong women <u>really turn me on</u>. It's <u>sweet</u> when a confident woman asks me out. I <u>hate</u> hanging out at home...having a few pints at the pub is <u>my favorite pastime</u> but a round of golf is all right too!

3. With your partner, explain the reasons for your choice to another pair.

<u>Homework:</u>

A. "Speaking" and "Journal" activities from <u>The Homework Book</u>
                    OR
B. Ask a native speaker (homestay family/friend/another teacher) about the habits and characteristics of a close friend or romantic partner.

TEACHER'S PAGES

Key:

Δ I am crazy about Δ I can't do without ◇ I love ◇ I really like Δ I can't get enough of O1 ___ is awesome	Δ I don't mind O2 ___ is alright/all right	Δ O3 I loathe ◇ I hate ◇ I can't stand Δ◇ I dislike Δ I'm not crazy about Δ2 I don't care for Δ I can live without Δ3 ___sucks

Δ CHALLENGES:

Δ   Students often neglect to use a gerund or noun phrase after a preposition

Δ2   Students sometimes confuse "care for" and "care about"

Δ3   Students tend to use "sucks" as an adjective and add a "be-verb" e.g. Grammar is sucks.

◇ GRAMMAR EXPANSION:

◇   Practice with gerunds and infinitives as direct objects

other: *Practice with coordinating conjunctions e.g. Neither Maria nor I care for shy people
*Practice with so/too/neither/either e.g. A: I can't stand burning rubber. B: Me neither!
*Practice with Y/N questions formation e.g. Do you like impulsive people?

O PRONUNCIATION:

O1   Some students struggle with the /ɔː/

O2   Some students struggle with the /l/ and /r/

O3   Some students struggle with the /ð/ and /z/ combination (loathes)

TEACHER'S PAGES

Teaching Ideas:

1 gambits
- ✓ elicit gambits from students prior to handing out gambit sheet; have a contest to see which team guesses the most from the list
- ✓ enlarge faces and place them around the room; cut gambits into separate squares or strips and have students race to place the appropriate gambits under the correct face.

2 warm-up
- ✓ students should circulate around the class; perhaps limit a "bingo" to five different students names in a row.
- ✓ time the game and the student with the most names written across the individual squares is the winner.
- ✓ give students time in pairs to share results and explore meaning

3 discussion
- ✓ pre-teach underlined vocabulary if necessary. Students can use drawing activities, charades, magazine scavenger hunts, etc... to guess or demonstrate meaning
- ✓ cut questions into strips and a) post them around the class or school for a "run-read-ask" relay or b) put the strips in a bag or basket or c) do a "strip-exchange", in which students each have one question and, after asking one student, exchange questions with him/her and move on to another student. Repeat until everyone has heard and asked almost all questions or d) organize students into two "speaking lines" facing each other. Have one line continuously move down after two facing students have asked each other their questions

context 1
- ✓ bring in "mystery smells" in bags or containers and blindfold students to guess what they are
- ✓ have students play "pictionary" or "charades" to depict smells
- ✓ an introduction to sensory verbs, e.g. I <u>smell</u> something <u>burning</u>.

context 2
- ✓ cut vocabulary and definitions in to separate strips and a) have partners match them (perhaps racing other partner teams) or b) have each student hold one strip and walk around repeating it to fellow classmates in order to find his/her "definition-partner"
- ✓ practice with adjective clauses, describing types, e.g. I like a person <u>who isn't too reserved</u>

PLANS AND INTENTIONS

What are you up to (tonight)?   *Anything going on (tonight)?*

WHAT ARE YOU DOING (TONIGHT)?

What do you feel like doing?   *ANY IDEAS ABOUT (TONIGHT)?*

Do you have any plans for (tonight)?

What do you intend/plan to do?

WHAT ARE YOU GOING TO DO?

Are you planning on___?

ASKING

Maybe I'll__   I WAS THINKING ABOUT__

I'm trying to decide between__ and __

I'm not sure what I'm going to do   **who knows?**

There's a chance I'll__   I might__

IT'S UP IN THE AIR RIGHT NOW

THINKING

I'M SUPPOSED TO __   I'm planning on__

I have plans to __ **I (don't) intend to__**   *I hope to__*

I'm going to __   I (don't) plan on __

I FIGURE I'LL __   MY PLAN IS TO__   what I'll do is__

I have no/every intention of __   **I'm definitely__**   **I'll probably__**

There's no doubt I'll___   I WILL HAVE__ BY__

STATING

PLANS AND INTENTIONS: TRUE OR FALSE SEARCH

1. With a partner, write a classmate's name (and your teacher's!) next to the activity you think they are likely to be doing on the weekend.

2. Use everybody's name at least once.

3. Go find out if you are right or wrong, using your "Intentions and Plans" (ASKING). Use STATING or THINKING to answer questions your classmates ask you.

   e.g. You (or your partner): Hey Marta, <u>what are you up to</u> this weekend?

   Marta: <u>I'm planning on</u> catching a movie.

CLASSMATE	WEEKEND ACTIVITY	T or F?
Marta	Getting drunk	F

4. The pair to get the most "TRUE" wins!

CLASSMATE	WEEKEND ACTIVITY	T or F?
	Get drunk	
	<u>Hit the books</u>	
	<u>Work out</u>	
	<u>Be a couch potato</u>	
	<u>Catch a flick</u>	
	Shop	
	<u>Pick up</u> a guy or girl	
	<u>Throw a party</u>	
	Cook	
	Hike	
	Sit at the computer	
	Sleep	
	<u>Pig out</u>	
	Play a sport	
	<u>Make out with</u> girl/boyfriend	
	Read	
	(you choose!)	
	(you choose!)	

*Your teacher will help you with some of the <u>underlined</u> expressions!

PLANS AND INTENTIONS: "Q & A" STUDENT CARDS

QUESTION: What are you up to this weekend?
I plan on
I'm supposed to
Maybe I'll

QUESTION: Do you have any plans for this weekend?
I'm going to
I figure I'll
I'll probably

QUESTION: What are you doing this weekend?
I hope to
I'm definitely
I intend to

QUESTION: Anything going on this weekend?
I was thinking about
There's a chance I'll
I have every intention of

QUESTION: What do you intend to do this weekend?
I have plans to
I might
I'm trying to decide between

QUESTION: What are you going to do this weekend?
My plan is to
(There's) no doubt I'll
I'm planning on

QUESTION: What do you feel like doing this weekend?
I hope to
I'm going to
I figure I'll

from *Function-all I: Intermediate Plus* by Fiona Bramble © Functionall Books 2006   www.eslenglish.ca

PLANS AND INTENTIONS

"A good traveler has no fixed plans and is not intent upon arriving"

Lao-Tzu (Li Erh), Founder of Taoism, (BC 600-?)

<u>Discussion Questions</u>:
In pairs or small groups, discuss the following:

1. Are you a "good traveler", according to Lao-Tzu? Why might having "no fixed plans" make one a good traveler? Do you live your life in the same way you 'travel'?

2. Fill in:

NOUN	plan	intention
VERB		
ADJECTIVE		
ADVERB		

   What is the difference between a "plan" and an "intention"?

3. What plans for your life do you think are <u>set in stone?</u>

4. What has probably happened when someone says "I did it <u>with the best of intentions</u>"?

5. What does a father mean when he says to his daughter's boyfriend, "What are <u>your intentions</u>?"

6. What special times of the year do you like to make plans? Or do you prefer to <u>play it by ear</u>?

7. Has anything recently <u>spoiled</u> or <u>wrecked</u> your plans? Explain.

8. Is it easy for you to <u>put your plans on hold</u> if something <u>comes up</u>? Why or why not?

9. What is the best experience you have had that <u>wasn't in the plan</u>?

10. What is your <u>master plan</u>?

OLD HABITS DIE HARD!
My <u>plans</u> for self-improvement

Pre-Discussion

1. In pairs or small groups, discuss which of the following areas in your life could use improvement (HOW & WHY!):

Body	*hair*	**time management**	GRADES
ENERGY	**work**	*ATTITUDE*	relationships
SEX	**wardrobe**	**SMOKING & DRINKING**	
car	**diet**	*SLEEP*	organization

2. Share your answers as a class

3. The following quiz tests how "connected" you are to people and the world around you. Take turns asking (ORALLY) each other the questions below. Record <u>your partner's</u> answers.

1. Do you make time to be with your family, even if it means giving up some activity you might enjoy? **Y/N**

2. Do you eat family dinner together with the family you've created or joined, or spend time together with them each day in some other way? **Y/N**

3. Do you know the people next door well enough to ask them to do you a favor? **Y/N**

4. Do you sometimes get so interested in your work that you forget what time it is or where you are? **Y/N**

5. Do you know details about your parents' and grandparents' lives? **Y/N**

6. Are there special natural places that you go to in order to think or relax? **Y/N**

7. Are you able to stop unimportant messages, <u>random data</u>, and useless information from <u>overwhelming</u> you? **Y/N**

8. Do you feel a connection to something greater than you, whether you call it God, the cosmos, or some other name? **Y/N**

9. Do you feel okay about your body? **Y/N**

*quiz adapted from "Are You Connected" by Edward M. Hallowell, MD

4. The "answers' to the quiz:

➤ **If you answered 7 or more questions "Yes":**

Congratulations! You enjoy a variety of strong human connections.

➤ **If you answered 7 or more questions "No":**

These results tell you what you may already know: You need to work on re-establishing lost relationships and establishing new ones.

➤ **If you answered "Yes" and "No" almost equally:**

You're connected to the world around you, but there's definitely room for improvement.

5. For the questions to which you answered "No", discuss with your partner, what you could change about your life to make those answers a "Yes".

e.g. #3: I could start saying "good morning" to my neighbours.

Function Practice:

1. Using your expressions from "Intentions and Plans", choose 1 or 2 areas of your life (from <u>Pre-Activity</u> #1 or #5) that you want to improve and tell your partner your short-term and long-term PLANS for improvement. You can write some notes below.

e.g. A: I really want to improve my GRADES.

B: <u>What are you going to do</u>?

A: Starting this week, <u>I'm going to study</u> an extra two hours.

B: Wow! <u>What else do you plan to do</u>?

A: Well, this month <u>I'm definitely learning</u> 100 new vocabulary words and <u>I have every intention of</u> only speaking English!

THIS WEEK	THIS MONTH	THIS YEAR
1.	1.	1.
2.	2.	2.
3.	3.	3.

2. Trade partners and tell your new partner about your first partner's plans!

Homework:

A. "Speaking" and "Journal" activities from <u>The Homework Book</u>

OR

B. Ask a native speaker (homestay family/friend/another teacher) the questions about his/her life in <u>Pre-discussion</u> #1 or from the "quiz" in <u>Pre-discussion</u> #3

♫ I'M LEAVING ON A JET PLANE ♪
Making traveling <u>plans</u>

Game:
1. In pairs or small groups, spend 10-15 minutes playing the "Geography Game". One person says a place name, then the next person says a place name starting with the last letter of the previous place and so on.

   e.g.   A: TrinindaD
                B: DenmarK
                C: KansaS
                A: SingaporE

   If you take longer than 20 seconds to respond, your partner or classmates can choose a punishment (like singing your national anthem in front of the class!) for you.

Pre-Discussion:
1. In pairs or small groups, look at the map below and talk about places you've been and places you'd like to go (LABEL THEM!)
2. Put an "X" on the places you've traveled to and describe each place in terms of its:

   a. ATTRACTIONS/ACTIVITIES   d. COSTS
   b. METHODS OF TRANSPORTATION   e. CLIMATE
   c. ACCOMMODATION   f. VISAS/SHOTS REQUIRED

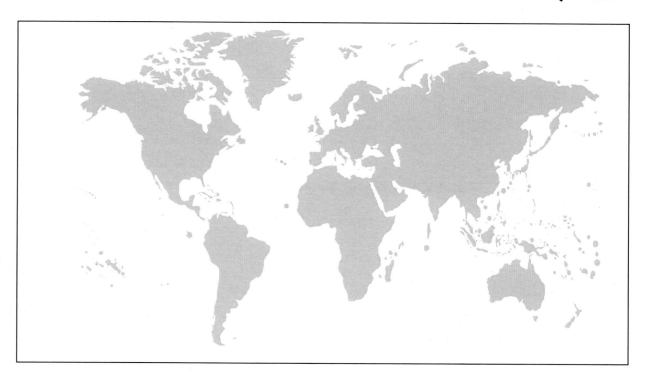

TRAVEL AGENT

Function Practice:

1. With another "travel agent", read and understand the
   DESTINATION CARDS your teacher will give you. Your teacher
   will help you with vocabulary.

2. Using your "Plans and Intentions" expressions, make a list of
   questions you can ask a traveler who is planning a trip. Consider:

LOCATION/CLIMATE	e.g. <u>Are you planning on</u> getting a tan?
ATTRACTIONS/ACTIVITIES	e.g. <u>Do you intend to</u> visit the Queen?
ACCOMMODATION	e.g. Where do you <u>hope to</u> stay?
LENGTH OF TIME	e.g. How long do you <u>plan to</u> stay?
COST	e.g. <u>Any ideas about</u> your budget?
TRANSPORTATION	e.g. How are you <u>going to</u> get around?
VISAS/SHOTS ETC…	e.g. When are you <u>getting</u> your visa?

_____

_____

_____

_____

_____

3. When "travel agents" and "travelers" are ready, travelers will
   come to speak to you and your partner about their travel PLANS.
   a. ask them your questions
   b. listen to them about their PLANS
   c. based on your conversation, try to "sell" ONE of your
      DESTINATIONS as a possibility and explain WHY.
      e.g. Because <u>you figure you'll</u> do some snorkelling and <u>you don't</u>
      <u>intend</u> to spend a lot of money, we recommend you go to___ .

4. After all "travelers" have spoken to all "travel agents", the
   "travelers" will explain to the class the one DESTINATION they
   chose and why.

Homework:
   A. "Speaking" and "Journal" activities from <u>The Homework Book</u>
                           OR
   B. Ask a native speaker (homestay family/friend/another teacher)
      about any upcoming travel plans he/she has and share yours.

TRAVELER

Function Practice:

1. With another "traveler", talk about two or three *types* (not necessarily a specific place) of places to which you want to travel.

2. Imagine you are planning a trip to one of these destinations and list some of your PLANS considering the aspects below:

	DESTINATION #1	DESTINATION #2
LOCATION/CLIMATE		
ATTRACTIONS/ACTIVITIES		
ACCOMODATION		
LENGTH OF TIME		
BUDGET		
TRANSPORTATION		

3. When "travelers" and "travel agents" are ready, you and your partner should visit each travel agent and, using your "Plans and Intentions" expressions,
   a. answer his/her questions
   b. talk about your PLANS
   c. record the destination each agent suggests for you and why he/she suggested it:

SUGGESTION	REASONS

4. After "travelers" have spoken to "travel agents", "travelers" must explain to the class the one DESTINATION they chose from the several suggestions and why, using "Plans and Intentions" expressions.

Homework:

A. "Speaking" and "Journal" activities from The Homework Book
OR
B. Ask a native speaker (homestay family/friend/another teacher) about any upcoming travel plans he/she has and share yours.

DESTINATION CARDS

RIO DE JANEIRO, BRAZIL
Climate: Tropical
Currency: 1 Real (R$1)= US$0.34
Cost of living:
3-course meal with wine/beer: R$20.
Attractions/Activities:
1. Copacabana: known for its amazing, wide, sandy beach that stretches for four kilometers
2. Maracanã: the epicentre of Brazilian football and a Mecca for sports fans
3. Popular bars and clubs: the beach communities of Copacabana, Ipanema and Leblon are good for a night out.
Accommodation:
Hotels: R$105-500
Transportation:
Air, bus
Visa requirements:
Visas can be obtained on arrival
Vaccinations/health:
Malaria

BOMBAY, INDIA
Climate: Temperatures can reach 52°C
Currency:
100 Indian Rupee (Rs100) = US$2.27
Cost of living:
3-course meal with beer/wine: Rs650-850
Attractions/Activities:
1. St Thomas's Cathedral
2. Town Hall
3. Chatrapati Shivaji Terminus (CST) was completed in 1888 for the Great Indian Peninsular Railway
4. Shrine of Haji Ali
5. Prince of Wales Museum
Accommodation
Hostels & Hotels: $50(US)-$250 (US)
Transportation:
Air, bus, train
Visa requirements:
Tourist visa obtained abroad
Vaccinations/health:
Typhoid, malaria

SOUTH ISLAND, NEW ZEALAND
Climate: Temperate climate.
Currency: NZ $1= US$ 0.60
Cost of living:
3-course meal with wine/beer: NZ $ 20
Attractions/Activities:
1. Rafting, canoeing, kayaking
2. Fishing
3. Jetskiing
4. Glacier walks
5. Gold-panning
Accommodation:
Luxury hotels to backpackers hostels for every budget.
Transportation:
Air, bus
Visa requirements:
Tourist visa obtained abroad
Vaccinations/health:
n/a

PRAGUE, CZECH REPUBLIC

NEPAL
Climate: From sub-tropical to arctic depending upon the altitude
Currency: 1 Nepalese Rupee (NPR) = US $ 0.01331
Cost of living:
You could live in Nepal on US$5 a day
Attractions/Activities:
1. Popular treks from Kathmandu include the Everest Base Camp, and the Helambu and Langtang treks.
Accommodation:
Backpacker inns and lodges
Transportation:
Few direct flights; Public buses are the main form of transportation
Visa requirements:
Visas can be obtained on arrival
Vaccinations/health:
The high altitude can cause insomnia, headaches, nausea, and altitude sickness

JAMAICA

DESTINATION CARDS

Climate: 0° C in winter to 25°C in summer **Currency**: 100.00 CZK (Czech Koruna) = US$ 4.34 **Cost of living**: 3-course meal with wine/beer: $8 US **Attractions/Activities**: 1. Architecture 2. Prague Castle 3. Bars and Clubs: a very exciting nightlife 4. Charles Bridge **Accommodation**: Backpackers' inns, apartments, hotels **Transportation**: Air, bus, train **Visa requirements**: Most travelers do not need a visa **Vaccinations/health**: n/a	**Climate**: Around 27-30°C **Currency**: 1 Jamaican Dollar (JMD) = US $0.01631 **Cost of living**: 3-course meal with wine/beer: $12 US **Attractions/Activities**: 1. Horseback riding 2. Golf 3. Scuba diving 4. Sailing 5. Caves **Accommodation**: Budget hotel: US$2-5, midrange hotel: US$5-20, top-end hotel: US$20 **Transportation**: Air, cruise ship, bus system is unreliable **Visa requirements**: Most travelers do not need a visa **Vaccinations/health**: Malaria

1. Each pair of "travel agents" can be given one or two cards, depending on class size. Each travel agent should try to "sell" his/her destination by matching it to the travelers' PLANS as much as possible.

2. Travel information is far from comprehensive; students should be encouraged to add any details they can!

TEACHER'S PAGES

Key:

ASKING

Δ1/◊/O What are you up to (tonight)?

Δ1/◊ Anything going on (tonight)?

Δ1/◊/O WHAT ARE YOU DOING (TONIGHT)?

O What do you feel like doing?

Δ1/◊/O1 Do you have any plans for (tonight)?

O What do you intend/plan to do?

O WHAT ARE YOU GOING TO DO?

O1 Are you planning on__?

THINKING

Δ2 Maybe I'll__

Δ I WAS THINKING ABOUT__

Δ2 I'm not sure what I'm going to do

Δ2 There's a chance I'll__

STATING

Δ I'm planning on__	◊1 I have plans to __
◊1 I (don't) intend to__	◊1 I hope to__
Δ2 I'm going to __ Δ I (don't) plan on__	Δ2 I FIGURE I'LL __
◊1 MY PLAN IS TO__ Δ2 what I'll do is__	Δ I have no/every intention of __
Δ2 I'm definitely__	Δ2 There's no doubt I'll___
Δ2 I'll probably__ Δ2 I WILL HAVE __ BY__	

Δ CHALLENGES:

Δ   Students struggle with the gerund phrase that can follow the preposition

Δ1   Prepositional phrases and time phrases are common here;
e.g. Anything going on <u>in the morning</u> ? or Any ideas about <u>the weekend</u>?

Δ2   Students struggle with future forms
  ➢ 'will' vs. 'be going to' ('will' is used for PLANS when used with a modifier,
    otherwise 'be going to' is more common for PLANS)
  ➢ future perfect
  ➢ present progressive (continuous) for future

◊ GRAMMAR EXPANSION:

◊   Practice with prepositional phrases and time phrases

◊1   Practice with infinitives as subject/noun complements or direct objects

ALL (STATING)   Practice with "will", "be going to", future perfect, present progressive for future

O PRONUNCIATION:

O   Reduction and linking patterns in wh-question formation, e.g. <u>What are you up to</u> (/wʌdəryə ʌptə/ or /wʌtʃyə ʌptuː/) tonight?

O1   In fast speech, 'you' is reduced to /yə/

TEACHER'S PAGES

Teaching Ideas:

1 gambits
- ✓ elicit gambits from students prior to handing out gambit sheet; have a contest to see which team guesses the most from the list.
- ✓ in pairs or groups, make students responsible for suggesting expressions belonging to only one gambit aspect (e.g. "ASKING").
- ✓ have students organize gambits into formal or informal groups on board.

2 warm-up
- ✓ students can "bet" (pennies/fake money) on answers and justify their answers.
- ✓ to wrap-up, you can write results in a chart on the board or copy the "SEARCH" chart onto an overhead and document student findings.
- ✓ "Q and A STUDENT CARDS" are optional but can give students focused practice. Students can exchange their card with another student each time they use it for more varied practice.

3 discussion
- ✓ pre-teach underlined vocabulary if necessary. Students can use drawing activities, charades, magazine scavenger hunts, etc… to guess or demonstrate meaning.
- ✓ cut questions into strips and a) post them around the class or school for a "run-read-ask" relay or b) put the strips in a bag or basket or c) do a "strip-exchange", in which students each have one question and, after asking one student, exchange questions with him/her and move on to another student. Repeat until everyone has heard and asked most questions.

context 1
- ✓ <u>Pre-discussion</u> can be done as a class on an overhead.
- ✓ there are many online personality quizzes, e.g. http://www.quizstop.com/
- ✓ collect PLANS from <u>Function Practice</u> from each student and read some aloud to class; get students to guess whose PLAN is whose and why.

context 2
- ✓ <u>Game</u> can be expanded by having students run to a wall map and point to or put a coloured pin on each previous place name stated. Having different countries or continents on different walls can add challenge and chaos. ☺
- ✓ Internet or book research can be done instead of or in addition to using "DESTINATION CARDS".
- ✓ students can prepare an oral presentation on a specific place as a follow-up activity.

94

REGRETS

I should (not) have__   How could I have been so stupid to__?

I MUST HAVE BEEN CRAZY TO__   I should have known better than to__

I could just shoot myself for (not)_   (IF) I COULD HAVE JUST__

Why didn't I __?   *If only I had (not)__*   **I CAN'T BELIEVE I__**

I wish I hadn't__   What (the hell*) was I thinking__?

I'LL NEVER FORGIVE MYSELF FOR__   *I regret__*

NO REGRETS

Oh well.   What's done is done.   *No pain no gain.*

IT WAS OUT OF MY HANDS.   **IT WASN'T MEANT TO BE.**   *What could I do?*

God works in mysterious ways.   (There's) no use crying over spilled milk.

I DIDN'T HAVE MUCH OF A CHOICE.   There's a reason for everything.

It wasn't up to me.   **You win some, you lose some**.   Shit happens.   **I tried.**

You snooze, you lose.   C'EST LA VIE.   Que sera sera.

What goes around, comes around.   *It all comes out in the wash.*

I DID MY BEST.   Nobody's perfect.   **I don't regret__**

*other emphatic expressions can be used; e.g. "the heck", "the f**k"

REGRETS: "LIFE GAMEBOARD"

START		I REGRET__	Go ahead 2 spaces	WHAT THE HELL WAS I THINKING WHEN__?	Miss one turn
I SHOULD HAVE KNOWN BETTER THAN TO__		I'LL NEVER FORGIVE MYSELF FOR__			Go back 9 spaces
I SHOULD NOT HAVE__		Go back 3 spaces			I WISH I HADN'T__
Go ahead 2 spaces		Miss one turn			I WISH I HAD___
Follow the arrow!				END	I CAN'T BELIEVE I ___!
I MUST HAVE BEEN CRAZY TO__		I SHOULD HAVE__	Go back 2 spaces		Take the Shortcut Pass
I COULD JUST SHOOT MYSELF FOR___					Take an extra turn
Take an extra turn					IF ONLY I HAD__
HOW COULD I HAVE BEEN SO STUPID TO__	Go ahead 2 spaces	IF I COULD HAVE JUST__	Take an extra turn	WHY DIDN'T I___?	

REGRETS: "LIFE CARDS"

MY EX-GIRL /BOYFRIEND	A GAME OR SPORT	MY PARENTS	FOOD	A RECENT MOVIE	MONEY
A LETTER OR AN EMAIL	A PET	A VACATION	A FRIEND	THIS CLASS	A JOB
CAR, BUS OR BIKE	A PUB OR RESTAURANT	MY ROOM	A DATE	YESTERDAY	MY GOVERNMENT
THE WEATHER	A PARTY	MY BODY	MY CLOTHES	A CEREMONY OR EVENT	LAUNDRY OR CHORES

Game Instructions:
1. Need: a. game tokens, coins, paperclips or anything to mark their places
   b. one die
   c. one "LIFE GAMEBOARD" and one set of "LIFE CARDS" (cut up) per group of 2-4 students
2. Players:
   1. high die roll goes first
   2. if player lands on a "regret" square, player chooses a "LIFE CARD" from the pile placed face down on the centre of the board and, using the "regret" prompt on the board, makes a sentence to match the "LIFE CARD"

   e.g.   "LIFE CARD" :   THE WEATHER
        "regret" prompt: I wish I hadn't__
               Player: <u>I wish I hadn't worn this thick sweater because it's so hot today!</u>

   3. if player doesn't land on a "regret" square, player should follow instructions on board.

3.   First player to the end wins!

REGRETS

"It's better to regret something you've done than to regret something you haven't done"

Unknown

Discussion Questions:
In pairs or small groups, discuss the following:

1. Do you agree with the quotation above? What is something you regret *not* doing?

2. Have you <u>burned any bridges</u> in your professional or personal life that you regret? Explain.

3. Have you said anything today that you regret and you wish you could <u>take back</u>? Explain.

4. What's the difference in meaning between "I <u>regret to say</u> that you are not invited" and "I <u>regret saying</u> that you are (or "were") not invited"?

5. Do you spend time regretting the past or do you prefer to <u>move on</u>?

6. Who in your family is best at making you feel <u>guilty</u>? Explain.

7. If you do something you regret immediately afterwards, do you attempt to <u>set things straight</u>?

8. Which politicians or celebrities could have expressed the following regrets:
    a. "I shouldn't have attacked Iraq"
    b. "I wish I hadn't been assassinated"
    c. "I can't believe I trusted my stock broker"
    d. "What the hell was I thinking when I kissed Angelina?"

9. How are these words different: "regret", "<u>remorse</u>" and "<u>disappointment</u>"?

10. Do you believe elderly people who say they have "no regrets" about their lives? Why or why not?

IF ONLY WE HADN'T INVITED CRAZY UNCLE JOE
Wedding Reception <u>Regrets</u>

<u>Introduction to Vocabulary:</u>

1.   In small groups or with a partner, match the wedding vocabulary to the pictures below:

        a. BOUQUET   b. LIMOUSINE   c. INVITATION

        d. VEIL   e. GROOM   f. GARTER

        g. WEDDING BANDS   h. UPDO   i. CUMMERBUND

_____

_____

_____

_____

_____

_____

_____

_____

_____

Pre-Activity:

1. In small groups or with a partner, choose 6 of the wedding checklist items below and list some of the problems brides and grooms can have in connection to the items.

   e.g.

Wedding item	Possible problems
alcohol	*not enough *too much

- ☐ Wedding dress
- ☐ Bouquets
- ☐ Tuxedos/Suits
- ☐ Bridesmaids dresses
- ☐ Music
- ☐ Wedding rings
- ☐ Guest List
- ☐ Wedding Vows

- ☐ Location
- ☐ Food
- ☐ Alcohol
- ☐ Photographs
- ☐ Hair & makeup
- ☐ Bridal Registry
- ☐ Decorations
- ☐ Transportation

Wedding Item	Possible Problems

2. Share some of your answers as a class!

GROOM

<u>Function Practice</u>:

1. **Read the following story to your "bride":**

   My wedding day was the best day of my life even though some things went wrong! First, <u>my dress was a bit too tight</u> and I couldn't breathe properly and <u>my bridesmaids looked like big purple grapes</u> in their outfits! Not only that, but <u>the bouquets were so big</u> we could barely lift them. I <u>mixed up my vows</u> and <u>my mascara ran</u> when I cried. At the reception, <u>the champagne was really warm</u> and then <u>the band showed up an hour late</u>. We got some great gifts but we were also given <u>four toasters</u>!

2. **Dictate the <u>underlined</u> parts to your "bride" and ask him/her to write down *exactly* what you say. Do NOT help your "bride" with spelling! Do NOT read each part more than twice.**

3. **When your "bride" is finished:**
   a. **allow him/her to compare his/her notes to your story**
   b. **ask the bride to use his/her "Regrets" expressions to reflect on the problems of the wedding day.**
      e.g. <u>My dress was a bit too tight</u>:   <u>I wish I hadn't eaten</u> so much at the rehearsal dinner

4. **Your "bride" will read a story to you. Write the dictation and the "groom's regrets below:**

DICTATION	REGRET

<u>Homework</u>:

A. **"Speaking" and "Journal" activities from <u>The Homework Book</u>**
   OR

B. **Ask a native speaker (homestay family/friend/another teacher) about a party or special event he/she planned and any regrets he/she has about what happened.**

BRIDE

1. **Read the following story to your "groom":**

   I had a great time on my wedding day but there were a few bad moments, that's for sure! First, <u>my cummerbund didn't match the groomsmen's</u> and during the ceremony, my bride started crying and I <u>didn't have any tissue!</u> I had borrowed my buddy's car for our "limousine", but <u>it was a mess and didn't have any gas in it</u>. The reception was great except that <u>Uncle Joe got really drunk and passed out.</u> <u>We ran out of beer</u>, so I had to go get some. When I was getting the beer, I <u>bumped into an old girlfriend and told her to come over</u>. My wife was really mad!

2. Dictate the <u>underlined</u> parts to your "groom" and ask him/her to write down *exactly* what you say. Do NOT help your "groom" with spelling! Do NOT read each part more than twice.

3. When your "groom" is finished:
   a. allow him/her to compare his/her notes to your story
   b. ask the groom to use his/her "Regrets" expressions to reflect on the problems of the wedding day.
      e.g. <u>My cummerbund didn't match</u>:   <u>I should have checked </u>my suit earlier.

4. Your "groom" will read a story to you. Write the dictation and the "bride's" regrets below:

DICTATION	REGRET

Homework:
A. "Speaking" and "Journal" activities from <u>The Homework Book</u>
                          OR
B. Ask a native speaker (homestay family/friend/another teacher) about a party or special event he/she planned and any regrets he/she has about what happened.

FOLLOW THE LEADER
<u>Regrets</u> in Decision Making

<u>Pre-discussion</u>:
In small groups or with a partner, discuss the following:

1. Are you a leader, or a follower? Explain.
2. Who do you <u>look up to</u> in your life? Why?
3. In society, who, generally, are <u>role models</u>?
4. What are the qualities of a good leader?
5. Why do leaders sometimes <u>fall from grace</u>?

<u>Function Practice</u>:
1. **Match the following leaders or role models to the "REGRET" they might have. Explain your choices.**

A. Politician   ___ I can't believe I let them off the hook on their homework!

B. Teacher   ___ Why didn't I listen to my advisor?

C. Coach   ___ I could just shoot myself for letting him off the bench!

D. Military leader   ___ I regret having to downsize.

E. Older sibling   ___ What the hell was I thinking bringing her to the party?

F. Parent   ___ I'll never forgive myself for sending them in there.

G. CEO   ___ I should have known better than to leave them alone!

2. **Discuss:**
    a. **the decision the leader or role model may have made**
    b. **the possible result of that decision**
        e.g.   Decision: The coach decided to use an average player
                Result: They lost the game

3. With your partner, using your "Regrets" expressions, decide which answers would best complete the chart below. Explain your choices!

CEO:

	#1	#2	#3
DECISION	lie to stockholders		Lay off employees
RESULT		go to jail	
REGRET		I should not have taken the money	
NO REGRET	What could I do?		

COACH:

	#1	#2	#3
DECISION	do a random drug test		change the strategy
RESULT		short one player	
REGRET	Why didn't I warn them?		
NO REGRET		Shit happens	

4. You and your partner should take the role of "CEO" or "COACH" and explain your decisions, the results, your regret and lack of regret in a short dialogue.

e.g.
COACH: I decided to do a random drug test.
PARTNER: Oh yeah, what happened?
COACH: Well, six of my players _____.
PARTNER: Oh no!
COACH: I know, why didn't I warn them?
PARTNER: Don't feel too bad.
COACH: Yeah, what could I do?

Homework:
A. "Speaking" or "Journal" activities from The Homework Book
OR
B. Speak to a native speaker (homestay family/friend/another teacher) who is a role model or leader. Ask him/her about some difficult decisions he/she has made and any regrets he/she may have about them.

Key:

REGRETS

Δ3/◊2/O I should (not) have__   Δ4/O1 *Why didn't I __?*   ◊1 *If only I had (not)__*

Δ3/Δ4/◊2/O/O1 *How could I have been so stupid to__?*   Δ3/◊2/O I MUST HAVE BEEN CRAZY TO__

Δ1/◊1 *I wish I hadn't__*   Δ3/◊2/O I should have known better than to__   Δ/◊ I regret__

Δ2 **I could just shoot myself for (not)_**   Δ2 I'LL NEVER FORGIVE MYSELF FOR__

Δ3/◊1/◊2/O (IF) I COULD HAVE JUST__   Δ4/O1 what (the hell*) was I thinking__?

NO REGRETS

Δ4 *What could I do?*   Δ5 C'EST LA VIE.   Δ5 Que sera sera.   Δ/◊ *I don't regret__*

Δ CHALLENGES:

Δ   Students struggle with choice of gerund or infinitive direct object
Δ1   Students struggle with past perfect structure following 'wish'
Δ2   Students struggle with gerund structure following the preposition
Δ3   Students often confuse modal perfects
   ➢ 'should': regret vs. expectation
   ➢ 'must': guessing/inference
   ➢ 'could': past possibility voiced as regret
Δ4   Students struggle with rhetorical aspect
Δ5   Students wonder about the use of other languages in "English" ☺

◊ GRAMMAR EXPANSION:

◊   Practice with infinitive vs. gerund
◊1   Practice with "3rd" conditional, particularly an implied conditional
◊2   Practice with modal perfects

O PRONUNCIATION:

O   Reduction in modal perfect forms e.g. should have done: /ʃʊdəv dʌn/ or /ʃʊdə dʌn/
O1   Intonation patterns for rhetorical 'questions'
ALL   As always, remind students of the linking, syllable reduction, word and sentence stress, and intonation patterns of English.

Teaching Ideas:

1 gambits
- ✓ elicit gambits from students prior to handing out gambit sheet; have a contest to see which team guesses the most from the list.
- ✓ have students organize gambits into formal and informal groups on board.

2 warm-up
- ✓ squares on game board can be written on individual full sheets of paper and placed on the floor for students to "walk" the game.
- ✓ you can put "LIFE CARDS" on an overhead to introduce the function by sharing your own regrets for some of the situations.
- ✓ **arrows** on gameboard confuse things a bit, but there is a way to get to the end regardless!

3 discussion
- ✓ pre-teach underlined vocabulary if necessary. Students can use drawing activities, charades, magazine scavenger hunts, etc… to guess or demonstrate meaning.
- ✓ cut questions into strips and a) post them around the class or school for a "run-read-ask" relay or b) put the strips in a bag or basket or c) do a "strip-exchange", in which students each have one question and, after asking one student, exchange questions with him/her and move on to another student. Repeat until everyone has heard and asked most questions.

context1
- ✓ pictures from Introduction to Vocabulary can be placed around the room and students can race to match the appropriate vocabulary.
- ✓ Pre-Activity can be done as a class.
- ✓ Function Practice #1 is great fun as a "running dick" (running dictation). A running dick can be done by:
  - a. sticking several "bride" and "groom" stories around the room and having each partner in each pair run to the story, read and remember as much as he/she can, then run back to partner and dictate what he/she remembers while the sitting partner writes it down. Repeat steps until the entire passage has been dictated. Other partner repeats process.
    #### OR, FOR ADDED FUN:
  - b. tape a "groom" or "bride" story to each student's back and write the name of another student on the top of each story. Each partner has to find his/her name on another's student's back and read the attached story, remember as much as he/she can, then run back to partner and dictate what he/she remembers while the sitting partner writes it down. Repeat steps until the entire passage has been dictated. Other partner repeats process.

context2
- ✓ as a good follow-up, sports movies such as "Coach Carter" with Samuel Jackson or "Jerry Maguire" with Tom Cruise reflect the difficulties in being a leader or role model and the decision making process. "Bedazzled" with Brendan Fraser and Elizabeth Hurley offers humourous insight into the concept of "be careful what you wish for". Students really enjoy it!

surprise & disbelief

informal

- ❖ Wow!
- ❖ Holy cow!
- ❖ Holy s**t!
- ❖ No way!
- ❖ Oh my gosh/god/goodness!
- ❖ Shut up!
- ❖ F**k off!
- ❖ Get out!
- ❖ Well, shut my mouth!
- ❖ Who would have thought!
- ❖ I never would have guessed!
- ❖ How about that!

- ◆ You've got to be kidding/joking
- ◆ You can't be serious
- ◆ Get out of here/town
- ◆ No way
- ◆ That's impossible
- ◆ Are you s**tting me?
- ◆ Who are you trying to kid?
- ◆ Shut up
- ◆ That's bulls**t/b.s.
- ◆ Give me a break
- ◆ Have another drink
- ◆ Yeah, sure
- ◆ Come on

formal

- ❖ I'm speechless
- ❖ I don't quite know what to say
- ❖ I'm dumbfounded
- ❖ What a (pleasant) surprise
- ❖ I had no idea
- ❖ That's unbelievable
- ❖ I didn't expect this at all

- ◆ I find that a little hard to swallow/to believe
- ◆ Where exactly did you get your information?
- ◆ Are you sure/certain?
- ◆ That doesn't support the information I have
- ◆ That runs contrary to current belief
- ◆ Where did you hear that?
- ◆ I've never heard that before
- ◆ That's a bit farfetched
- ◆ I can't believe that___

SURPRISE AND DISBELIEF: THE NO WAY GAME

1. Get out of your seat! Stand in the middle of the room!
2. Your teacher or another classmate will read the information below
3. If you think a fact is:
   a. SURPRISING but TRUE: run to the right wall of the classroom and shout: NO WAY!   (rising intonation, raised eyebrows)
   b. SURPRISING but UNTRUE: run to the left wall of the classroom and shout: NO WAY (longer vowels, falling intonation)
4. Practice the different intonation patterns right now with your teacher

"FACTS":

1. In 2002, 70,000 Australians listed their religious beliefs as "Jedi".

2. An American teacher was fired for using a banana in the classroom to demonstrate condom use.

3. A chicken once had its head cut off and lived for over eighteen months, headless.

4. American Airlines saved $40,000 in 1987 by taking out one olive from each salad served in first class.

5. Approximately 40% of the U.S. paper money in circulation was counterfeit by the end of the Civil War.

6. Of all the restaurants that are opened, 90% of them fail in the first year.

7. Finland has 187,888 lakes and 179,584 islands.

8. Hitler was voted Time Magazine's man of the year in 1938.

9. In 1998, Sony accidentally sold 700,000 camcorders that had the technology to see through people's clothes.

10. 53% of women in America would dump their boyfriend if they did not get them anything for Valentine's Day.

11. Close to 73% of girls in Bangladesh are married by age 18.

12. Of married couples, 70% of men and 60% of women have cheated on their spouse.

SURPRISE AND DISBELIEF

WILEY@NON-SEQUITUR.NET   DIST. BY UNIVERSAL PRESS SYND.   WWW. NON-SEQUITUR.NET

NON SEQUITUR © 2000 Wiley Miller. Dist. By UNIVERSAL
PRESS SYNDICATE. Reprinted with permission. All rights reserved.

Discussion Questions:

In pairs or small groups, discuss the following:

1. What does the comic strip suggest about "the element of surprise"? Are surprises always good?

2. Do you like to be surprised? Explain.

3. What is a <u>practical joke</u>? Do you like to play practical jokes on others? Have you ever been the victim of a practical joke?

4. In what ways can "surprise" and "disbelief" be the same? In what ways can they be different? Show your partner what your face looks like when you are surprised by something and what you look like when you don't believe something you see or hear.

5. Do you usually <u>take people at face value</u>? Why or why not?

6. Who is the most <u>gullible</u> person you know? The most <u>skeptical</u>?

7. What types of people (e.g. politicians) should you <u>take with a grain (or "pinch") of salt</u>? Why?

8. What is something you tell people about yourself that always surprises them?

9. Which one of your friends likes to shock you or <u>pull your leg</u> on a regular basis with his/her crazy stories? Are you that friend? ☺

10. Do you believe anything is possible? Explain.

I HEARD IT THROUGH THE GRAPEVINE
Surprise and Disbelief when Gossiping

Pre-Activity:

1. In small groups or as a class, mark the activities below that you think your *teacher* could have done or does now.

☐ Bungee jump naked   ☐ Steal/shoplift

☐ Smoke marijuana   ☐ Flirt

☐ Sing or play in a band   ☐ Make out

☐ Lose his/her temper   ☐ Swear at his/her parents

☐ Get arrested   ☐ Cheat on an exam

2. Your teacher will try to convince you that he/she has done or does ALL of the activities above. After he/she has told a short story about each one, you must respond with either a "SURPRISE" or "DISBELIEF" expression *and* a reason why!

     e.g.   TEACHER: I once got arrested for peeing behind a tree in the park
           STUDENT: <u>Get out</u>! I can't imagine you doing that!
                  Surprise   **OR**
                  <u>Give me a break.</u> You wouldn't get arrested for THAT!
                  Disbelief

3. After your teacher's stories and your responses, your teacher, *if he/she wants to*, can tell you the truth!

Function Practice:

1. Tell your partner "2 truths and a lie", that is, 2 facts that are true about your life and 1 that isn't. Your partner will write your "truths" down.

2. Try to convince your partner that all 3 facts are true using as many details as possible. Your partner may ask questions as well.

3. Your partner will tell you which one they think is *not true* by using a "DISBELIEF" expression.

4. Your partner will tell you "2 truths and a lie". Write your partner's name, the "truths", and some of the details on the paper your teacher gives you.

e.g.

NAME	"TRUTH"	DETAILS
Young ho	He had dinner with a member of the royal family	-in 1999 -he was his dad's boss' friend

5. Use a "DISBELIEF" expression after you hear the 1 "truth" and details you *don't believe*.

6. Your teacher will give you a pair of scissors to cut each "truth" into separate strips. Your teacher will collect the strips, mix them up and give you three "truths" about your other classmates.

7. Using your "SURPRISE AND DISBELIEF" expressions, move around the room and gossip about your other classmates.

    e.g. A: Did you know that Young Ho has had dinner with royalty?
       B: <u>Yeah, sure</u>
       A: No really, his dad's boss is friends with a prince!
       B: <u>Come on</u>. When was this?
       A: Really! They all went for dinner in 1999.
       B: <u>Wow!</u>

To introduce the gossip you can use:

> Did you hear that...?
> Did you know...?
> I just found out that...
> I just heard that...

8. If there is time, you can share some of the best gossip as a class and guess which stories are true or not!

<u>Homework</u>:
    A. "Speaking" and "Journal" activities from <u>The Homework Book</u>
                OR
    B. Ask a native speaker (homestay family/friend/another teacher) to tell you something about themselves that usually surprises other people. Tell him/her something about you (or your classmates ☺) too!

SURPRISE AND DISBELIEF: GOSSIP CARDS

NAME	"TRUTH"	DETAILS

NAME	"TRUTH"	DETAILS

NAME	"TRUTH"	DETAILS

GROUP A

Pre-activity:

1. Ask your partner if he/she knows his/her country's:

a. WETTEST REGION:

b. MOST DENSELY POPULATED AREA:

c. HOTTEST YEAR:

d. MOST FAMOUS INVENTION:

e. WORST STORM:

f. RAREST ANIMAL:

g. MOST COMMON CAUSE OF DEATH:

h. LARGEST BODY OF WATER:

2. Share some of your answers as a class.

Function Practice:

1. "GROUP A" students and "GROUP B" students should sit in separate groups. Bring your "Surprise and Disbelief" expressions.

2. You and your group must guess the answers to the following science-related questions:

TOPIC	QUESTION
WEATHER	How many people were killed in history's most destructive hailstorm?
SPACE	What is the best-mapped planet in the solar system?
MOLECULES	How small are the smallest viruses?
ANIMALS	How much did the world's heaviest dog weigh?
PLANTS	What plant contains the most caffeine?
EARTH SCIENCES	What was the longest distance traveled by an audible sound?
INVENTIONS	Who invented the first robotic orchestra?
MEDICINE/HEALTH	What public health problem is the biggest killer of Americans?
TECHNOLOGY	When was the first fax patent issued?

3. Choose 1 person to read the answers when your teacher gives them to you. Respond to the answers with your "Surprise and Disbelief" expressions.

4. Follow the instructions for the "SUPERLATIVE QUIZ SHOW" on your answer key.

Homework:

A. "Speaking" and "Journal" activities from The Homework Book

OR

B. Ask a native speaker (homestay family/friend/ another teacher) the questions from Pre-Activity. Respond with your "Surprise and Disbelief" expressions.

WHO WOULD'VE THOUGHT THAT HAWAII GETS THE MOST RAIN!
Surprise and Disbelief in Science

GROUP B

Pre-activity:
1. Ask your partner if he/she knows his/her country's:
   a. WETTEST REGION:
   b. MOST DENSELY POPULATED AREA:
   c. HOTTEST YEAR:
   d. MOST FAMOUS INVENTION:
   e. WORST STORM:
   f. RAREST ANIMAL:
   g. MOST COMMON CAUSE OF DEATH:
   h. LARGEST BODY OF WATER:

2. Share some of your answers as a class.

Function Practice:
1. "GROUP A" students and "GROUP B" students should sit in separate groups. Bring your "Surprise and Disbelief" expressions.

2. You and your group must guess the answers to the following science-related questions:

TOPIC	QUESTION
WEATHER	What was the hottest outside temperature recorded?
SPACE	What is the most volcanically explosive planet in our solar system?
MOLECULES	What is the roundest molecule?
ANIMALS	Which animal has killed the most humans?
PLANTS	What tree is struck by lightning most often?
EARTH SCIENCES	Where is the world's clearest body of water?
INVENTIONS	What were the first envelopes made of?
MEDICINE/HEALTH	What hobby causes the greatest hearing loss?
TECHNOLOGY	What is the size of the world's smallest battery?

3. Choose 1 person to read the answers when your teacher gives them to you. Respond to the answers with your "Surprise and Disbelief" expressions.

4. Follow the instructions for the "SUPERLATIVE QUIZ SHOW" on your answer key.

Homework:
A. "Speaking" and "Journal" activities from The Homework Book
                    OR
B. Ask a native speaker (homestay family/friend/ another teacher) the questions from Pre-Activity. Respond with your "Surprise and Disbelief" expressions.

GROUP A

TOPIC	QUESTION
WEATHER	How many people were killed in history's most destructive hailstorm? **230**
SPACE	What is the best-mapped planet in the solar system? **VENUS**
MOLECULES	How small are the smallest viruses? **18 NANOMETERS**
ANIMALS	How much did the world's heaviest dog weigh? **343 LBS.**
PLANTS	What plant contains the most caffeine? **S. AMERICAN HOLLY**
EARTH SCIENCES	What was the longest distance traveled by an audible sound? **4600 KMS.**
INVENTIONS	Who invented the first robotic orchestra? **TAITO CORP. (JAPAN)**
MEDICINE/HEALTH	What public health problem is the biggest killer of Americans? **SMOKING**
TECHNOLOGY	When was the first fax patent issued? **1843**

Quiz Show Instructions:

1. Your "team" (A) asks the other team (B) your science questions. If:
   a. they answer correctly, respond with a "Surprise" expression and give them one point
   b. they answer incorrectly, respond with a "Disbelief" expression but give them a chance to explain their answer. If it is a good explanation, give them half a point.

GROUP B

TOPIC	QUESTION
WEATHER	What was the hottest outside temperature recorded? **158.8° F**
SPACE	What is the most volcanically explosive planet in our solar system? **VENUS**
MOLECULES	What is the roundest molecule? **C60 (PURE CARBON)**
ANIMALS	Which animal has killed the most humans? **MOSQUITOES**
PLANTS	What tree is struck by lightening most often? **OAK**
EARTH SCIENCES	Where is the world's clearest body of water? **LAKE MASHU, JAPAN**
INVENTIONS	What were the first envelopes made of? **MUD**
MEDICINE/HEALTH	What hobby causes the greatest hearing loss? **GUN-SHOOTING**
TECHNOLOGY	What is the size of the world's smallest battery? **100²NANOMETERS**

Quiz Show Instructions:

1. Your "team" (B) asks the other team (A) your science questions. If:
   a. they answer correctly, respond with a "Surprise" expression and give them one point
   b. they answer incorrectly, respond with a "Disbelief" expression but give them a chance to explain their answer. If it is a good explanation, give them half a point.

TEACHER'S PAGES

Key: surprise & disbelief

informal

❖ Wow!	◇2 You can't be serious
❖ Holy cow!	◇/O1 Get out of here/town
❖ Holy s**t!	O1 No way
❖ No way!	◇1/◇2 That's impossible
❖ Oh my gosh/god/goodness!	Δ/O Are you s**tting me?
◇/O1 Shut up!	Δ/O Who are you trying to kid?
◇/O1 F**k off!	◇/O1 Shut up
◇/O1 Get out!	◇1 That's bulls**t/b.s.
◇ Well, shut my mouth!	◇ Give me a break
❖ Who would have thought!	◇ Have another drink
❖ I never would have guessed!	O Yeah, sure
◇1 How about that!	◇ Come on

formal

◇2 I'm speechless	◇1 I find that a little hard to swallow/to believe
◇2 I'm dumbfounded	◇1 That doesn't support the information I have
◇1/◇2 That's unbelievable	◇1 That runs contrary to current belief
	Δ/O Where did you hear that?
	◇1 I've never heard that before
	◇1/◇2 That's a bit farfetched

Δ CHALLENGES:

Δ   Students may struggle with the rhetorical aspect

◇ GRAMMAR EXPANSION:

◇   Practice with imperatives

◇1   Practice with "that" as a referent

◇2   Practice with adjectives (those related to "surprise and disbelief" function)

Note: Context 2 is an appropriate context for practice with superlative structures (see Teaching Ideas)

O PRONUNCIATION:

O   Intonation patterns for rhetorical 'questions' and/or sarcasm

O1   It is important to contrast the intonation patterns of surprise and disbelief, e.g. shut↗ up↗ (surprise) shut↘ up↘ (disbelief) as well as the longer vowels that may be associated with disbelief expressions. Of course these patterns may not be used in your region

ALL (SURPRISE/informal)   Intonation patterns of exclamations

ALL   As always, remind students of the linking, syllable reduction, word and sentence stress, and intonation patterns of English.

Quiz Board (for board or overhead) context2

WEATHER	*SPACE*	**MOLECULES**
ANIMALS	**PLANTS**	EARTH SCIENCES
INVENTIONS	MEDICINE & HEALTH	TECHNOLOGY

TEACHER'S PAGES

Teaching Ideas:

1 gambits

- ✓ elicit gambits from students prior to handing out gambit sheet; have a contest to see which team guesses the most from the list.
- ✓ in pairs or groups, make students responsible for suggesting expressions belonging to only one gambit aspect (e.g. "SURPRISE/informal").
- ✓ have students organize gambits into formal or informal groups on board.

2 warm-up

- ✓ you may want to pre-teach vocabulary from "FACTS".
- ✓ you could cut "FACTS" into strips and have different students read them, perhaps the "losing" student (the one who goes left instead of right and vice versa!).
- ✓ for lower levels, perhaps use Pre-Activity from context1 instead of the "FACTS" and use your name or students' names as the subject, e.g. Min Jung cheated on her last exam.
- ✓ model the "No way" pattern several times.
- ✓ "FACTS" are all true!

3 discussion

- ✓ bring in and talk about or play some practical jokes on the students!
- ✓ pre-teach underlined vocabulary if necessary. Students can use drawing activities, charades, magazine scavenger hunts, etc... to guess or demonstrate meaning.
- ✓ cut questions into strips and a) post them around the class or school for a "run-read-ask" relay or b) put the strips in a bag or basket or c) do a "strip-exchange", in which students each have one question and, after asking one student, exchange questions with him/her and move on to another student. Repeat until everyone has heard and asked most questions.

context1

- ✓ as a follow-up, a good classroom project is writing/creating a tabloid newspaper, using the "gossip" students have gathered. Ask them to bring in pictures of themselves to use in the tabloid.
- ✓ "real" tabloids are also a great source of hard to swallow stories!
- ✓ www.yahoo.com has a section called "Oddly Enough" for unusual stories.

context2

- ✓ don't give answers to groups until they have spent 10-15 minutes in discussion.
- ✓ you can add to the quiz questions for a longer game. *The Guinness Book of World Records* is a good source. There are a number of trivia sites as well, e.g. http://www.angelfire.com/ca6/uselessfacts/
- ✓ this context lends itself well to the superlative structure for grammar expansion
- ✓ the "Quiz Board" in the Teacher's Pages can be copied onto the blackboard or used as an overhead to simulate a "Jeopardy"-type game. Instead of winning points, each topic could have a monetary value assigned.

*Note: It is true that students may not actually be surprised or doubtful of some of the information in the quiz, but encourage them to just have fun and "act" surprised!

worry

Something's just not right   I worry about/that___

I've got a bad feeling about this   **My stomach's in knots**

I'M NERVOUS ABOUT___   *I'm afraid to ___*   I'M RELUCTANT TO___

There are so many things that could go wrong

I have some concerns about___   **It's easier said than done**

I'M WORRIED (SICK) ABOUT/THAT___

I'm feeling pretty anxious about___   I have doubts about___

I have serious reservations about___

Reassurance

Don't stress

Everything will be all right

It's not as bad as you think   *It'll be fine*   IT'S ALL GOOD

RELAX

You can do it!   It's not a big deal

I have faith in you   *Don't work yourself up!*   It'll be worth it

It'll be over before you know it

No pain no gain   **You'll figure something out**

It'll all come out in the wash

There's nothing to worry about

from *Function-all 1: Intermediate Plus* by Fiona Bramble © Functionall Books 2006   www.eslenglish.ca

WORRY AND REASSURANCE: GO FISH

How do you feel about getting old?	<u>I worry that</u> I'll be too dependent on my family.
Are you ready for the test tomorrow?	<u>I'm worried</u> my mind will go blank.
What's going on with your travel plans?	<u>I'm feeling pretty anxious about</u> flying.
How's your Mom?	<u>I worry about</u> her health.
Are you ready for your blind date?	<u>I'm nervous about</u> going out with a complete stranger.

WORRY AND REASSURANCE: GO FISH

How are the kids?	<u>I've got a bad feeling about</u> their report cards.
How do feel about the state of the world?	<u>I'm pretty anxious about</u> the future.
What's going on with your new job?	<u>My stomach's in knots</u> every morning.
How's the diet?	<u>I have doubts about</u> whether it's working or not.
Are you buying that house?	<u>I have some serious reservations about</u> the area.

WORRY AND REASSURANCE: GO FISH

Are you ready for your presentation?	<u>I'm afraid</u> I'll get stage fright.
How's your boy/girlfriend?	<u>I'm reluctant</u> to get too serious.
What do you think about English class?	<u>I have some concerns</u> about my progress.

Game Instructions:
1. Copy, cut, and shuffle a set of cards for every pair of students
2. Each student holds four cards and the rest are placed face down in a pile
3. Like "Go Fish", one student reads one of his/her cards aloud to his/her partner. If the partner:
   a. thinks he/she has a match to the card (an answer or reply for the same context), he/she must read, then give the card to the other student. That student now has 1 pair and takes another turn
   b. doesn't think he/she has a match to the card, he/she says "Go Fish" and his/her partner takes a card from the pile
4. Each student should have four cards at all times, picking up from the pile when necessary, until the center pile is gone
5. The first student "out" of cards ends the game
6. The student with the most pairs wins

from *Function-all 1: Intermediate Plus* by Fiona Bramble © Functionall Books 2006   www.eslenglish.ca

WORRY AND REASSURANCE

"Don't worry about the world coming to an end today. It's already tomorrow in Australia."

Charles Schultz, "Peanuts" cartoonist (1922-2000)

Discussion Questions:
In pairs or small groups, discuss the following:

1. What does the quotation above mean? Do you like it? Why or why not? Do you like Snoopy?

2. Do you consider yourself a <u>worry wart</u>? If so, what do you usually worry about?

3. How do you relax after you've <u>gotten you worked up</u> about something?

4. What's the difference between "I worry" and "I'm worried"? Finish these sentences: I worry about _____
   I'm worried about_____

5. Are you good at reassuring other people when they are worried or <u>anxious</u>? What do you say or do to make them feel better?

6. If someone says "Don't be <u>paranoid</u>", what does he/she mean?

7. Which of your friends or family members tend to <u>make a mountain out of a molehill</u>?

8. Which of the following "worries" are you NOT likely to <u>lose any sleep over</u>? Explain why or why not.
   a. aging
   b. money
   c. personal safety
   d. job
   e. social status
   f. world affairs

9. What are some physical signs of worry? (e.g. bags under your eyes)

10. Who is worried about YOU right now? Why?

I'M AFRAID HE'LL NEVER SETTLE DOWN
Parenting <u>Worries</u>

ADULT

ADOLESCENT	CHILD	TODDLER	INFANT	FETUS

_____   _____   _____   _____   _____

_____   _____   _____   _____   _____

_____   _____   _____   _____   _____

_____   _____   _____   _____   _____

<u>Pre-activity</u>:

1. In small groups or with a partner, discuss what you remember of your life (or what your parents have told you!) at the different stages listed above.

2. In the lines below each stage, write a few of the typical experiences connected to each one, e.g. ADOLESCENT: first kiss

3. Share some of your answers as a class!

<u>Function Practice</u>:

1. Consider some of the experiences you wrote down in <u>Pre-Activity</u>. Which of them are situations YOU worried about and which ones are situations PARENTS might have worried about? Tell your partner.

    e.g. ADOLESCENT: <u>I was nervous about</u> my first kiss but <u>my parents were probably anxious</u> about me graduating!

2. **With your partner, discuss what worries parents might have in connection to the following:**

   a. their children's health
   b. their children's education
   c. their children's behaviour
   d. their children's personality
   e. their children's friends
   f. their children's family relationships
   g. their children's abilities/interests

3. **Imagine you are a parent of a child at every stage of development (including adulthood!). Using the topics above, tell your partner what you worry about. Use as many different " "Worry" expressions as you can!**

   e.g.

STAGE	TOPIC	WORRY
fetus	health	I'm anxious about eating the right things
adult	health	I'm worried he/she isn't eating well

4. **Your partner will now share his/her parenting worries with you. Use your "Reassurance" expressions and *a reason* to help him/her feel better!**

   e.g.   Your Partner: <u>I'm worried</u> he's not eating well

           You: <u>Don't work yourself up</u>; he knows how to take care of himself.

5. **Based on your partner's "worries" and method of "reassurance", rate him/her:**

   1 • 2 • 3 • 4 • 5 • 6 • 7 • 8 • 9 • 10
   (relaxed)   (worry wart)

   1 • 2 • 3 • 4 • 5 • 6 • 7 • 8 • 9 • 10
   (not reassuring)   (reassuring)

Homework

A. "Speaking" and "Journal" activities from <u>The Homework Book</u>
   OR
B. Talk to a native speaker (homestay family/friend/another teacher) who is a parent and ask about his/her parenting worries. Try to reassure him/her too!

$ MONEY MONEY MONEY $
Financial <u>Worries</u>

<u>Pre-Discussion</u>:

In small groups or with a partner, discuss the following:

1. In many cultures, even families, money is considered a <u>taboo</u> subject. Why do you think this is so? What about in your culture or family?
2. Describe your own <u>spending habits</u>.
3. Compare <u>the cost of living</u> in your country to that of another country.
4. Are you currently <u>on a tight budget</u>?
5. Think of two recent purchases you have made. Were they a <u>waste of money</u> or were they <u>worth it</u>? Explain.

<u>Function Practice</u>:

1. **With your partner, compare what your monthly or yearly budget is for the following items:**

Utilities	BEAUTY	transportation	**TRAVELLING & HOLIDAYS**
Debt	**entertainment**	*gifts*	jewelry	EMERGENCIES
TAXES	rent/mortgage	*FURNITURE*	*health*
Clothing	*education*	CHARITY	**food**	sports

Which items do you think you spend too much on? _____

_____

_____

_____

2. **How do you and your partner earn your money? (Circle which source(s))**

   a. JOB   c. ALLOWANCE   e. PANHANDLING
   b. SCHOLARSHIP/GRANT   d. LOAN   f. TRUST FUND

3. How much do you think is enough to save for:
    EDUCATION   _____
    BUYING A HOUSE/APARTMENT   _____
    RETIREMENT   _____
    RAISING A FAMILY   _____
    EMERGENCIES   _____
    A HOLIDAY   _____
    A CAR   _____

4. Your teacher will give you and your partner 1 "WORRY CARD" each. Thinking about the information in #1, #2, and #3, write one worry for each category like the examples below. DO NOT use a "Worry" expression!

	SPENDING WORRIES	EARNING WORRIES	SAVING WORRIES
Partner #1	name: Jorge	Name: Jorge	Name: Jorge
	can't afford my new textbook	I get paid minimum wage	I'll need ____ for retirement

	SPENDING WORRIES	EARNING WORRIES	SAVING WORRIES
Partner #2	name: Mika	Name: Mika	Name: Mika
	going out for dinner too much	my allowance is really small	trip to Whistler costs $3000!

5. Join another pair and exchange "WORRY CARDS".

6. Taking turns, report the new pairs' "worries" to your partner, using your "Worry" expressions. Respond to the worry with "Reassurance" and a good reason.

    e.g.   You (to your partner):   <u>Jorge is concerned about</u> how he's going to buy his new textbook.

           Your Partner (to Jorge):   <u>Relax.</u> You hate grammar anyway!

           Your Partner (to you):   <u>Mika is afraid</u> to ask her parents for more money.

           You (to Mika):   <u>You can do it!</u> Your parents want to help out!

7. When your group has finished sharing worries and reassuring each other, tell the other pair how well they reassured you by saying:

    Thanks. I feel a lot better now!   **OR**   I'm even more worried now!

<u>Homework</u>:
    A. "Speaking" and "Journal" activities from <u>The Homework Book</u>
                          OR
    B. Ask a native speaker (homestay family/friend/another teacher) what he/she is *saving* (#3) for and what worries he/she may have about it!

WORRY AND REASSURANCE: WORRY CARDS

SPENDING WORRIES	EARNING WORRIES	SAVING WORRIES
name:	name:	name:
worry:	worry:	worry:

✂

SPENDING WORRIES	EARNING WORRIES	SAVING WORRIES
name:	name:	name:
worry:	worry:	worry:

✂

SPENDING WORRIES	EARNING WORRIES	SAVING WORRIES
name:	name:	name:
worry:	worry:	worry:

✂

SPENDING WORRIES	EARNING WORRIES	SAVING WORRIES
name:	name:	name:
worry:	worry:	worry:

✂

SPENDING WORRIES	EARNING WORRIES	SAVING WORRIES
name:	name:	name:
worry:	worry:	worry:

✂

SPENDING WORRIES	EARNING WORRIES	SAVING WORRIES
name:	name:	name:
worry:	worry:	worry:

Key:

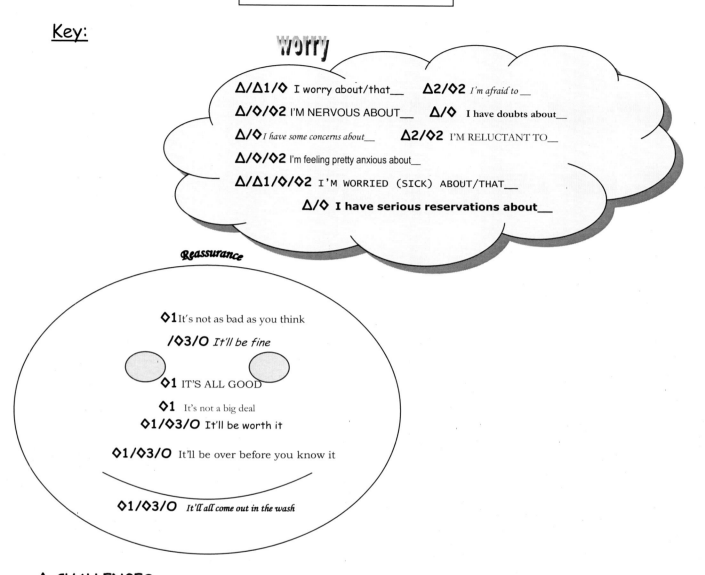

Δ CHALLENGES:

Δ Students struggle with the gerund, noun phrase or clause structure that follows the preposition

Δ1 Students struggle with "worry" vs. "worried"

Δ2 Students struggle with the preposition "to" vs. infinitive "to"

◊ GRAMMAR EXPANSION:

◊ Practice with gerunds, noun phrases and clauses

◊1 Practice with "it" as a referent

◊2 Practice with adjectives (those related to "worry" function)

◊3 Practice with "will" for future promises

ALL (WORRY) Practice with simple present

O PRONUNCIATION:

O linking and reduction (/t/ → /d/) e.g. It'll → / Idt/

ALL As always, remind students of the linking, syllable reduction, word and sentence stress, and intonation patterns of English.

Teaching Ideas:

1 gambits
- ✓ elicit gambits from students prior to handing out gambit sheet; have a contest to see which team guesses the most from the list.
- ✓ in pairs or groups, make students responsible for suggesting expressions belonging to only one gambit aspect.
- ✓ have students identify and discuss idiomatic expressions (e.g. "It'll all come out in the wash").

2 warm-up
- ✓ ask students to add a reassurance expression if they think the two cards are a match.
- ✓ you must circulate quickly to check matches.
- ✓ as a wrap-up or expansion, elicit from class the general topics of each match (e.g. "aging" or "school") and get students to ask extra questions to draw out "worries". Questions tend to start with: How do you feel about…?/ How is/are…?/ Are you…What's going on with…?/ What do you think about…?

3 discussion
- ✓ pre-teach underlined vocabulary if necessary. Students can use drawing activities charades, magazine scavenger hunts, etc… to guess or demonstrate meaning.
- ✓ cut questions into strips and a) post them around the class or school for a "run-read-ask" relay or b) put the strips in a bag or basket or c) do a "strip-exchange", in which students each have one question and, after asking one student, exchange questions with him/her and move on to another student. Repeat until everyone has heard and asked most questions.

context 1
- ✓ Pre-Activity can be done as a class on an overhead or perhaps each "stage" can be posted around the room.
- ✓ some family sitcoms ("Malcolm in the Middle"/"That 70's Show") or movies ("Meet the Parents"/ "Meet the Fockers") are a great introduction or follow-up for parental worries.

context 2
- ✓ empty your purse or wallet and show your bills and receipts to introduce spending habits.
- ✓ "Worry Cards" can be cut up and placed around the room; other students can write messages of reassurance below.
- ✓ instead of using "Worry Cards", pairs can just have a discussion of their money worries and reassure each other.
- ✓ find the average cost of the items in #3 in your country for discussion/comparison.

Classroom English

PRONUNCIATION

How do you pronounce this word?   *What is the pronunciation of this word?*

HOW DO YOU SAY THIS?   *I don't think we have this sound in my language*

This sound is really hard for me to make   Could you pronounce this for me?

REQUESTS

Do you mind repeating that?

COULD I GET SOME EXTRA HELP?

Is it o.k. if I go to the bathroom?

Can I translate it for him/her?

Can I use my dictionary?

Can I talk to you after class?

ASSISTING

Can I give you a hand with that?

Would you like to borrow my dictionary?

Do you want to change seats?

Do you have enough room?

Can you see o.k.?

Do you need to borrow a pencil/pen?

AM I IN YOUR WAY?

Can I help at all?

MEANING

What is the meaning of ___?

WHAT DOES ___MEAN?

Does ___ have more than one meaning ?

SPELLING
How do you spell___?
Is this spelled right?
What is the spelling of ___?

135

FUNCTIONS AND TOPICS   **PAGE NUMBER**

WARM-UP ACTIVITIES/GAMES	UNIT	PAGE
Jigsaw	Breaking up and Making up	3-4
Idiom Quiz	Checking Understanding	15
Debate Cards	Debate and Discussion	25-26
TIC-TAC-TOE Cards	Exaggeration	41-43
Mugshots	Guessing	55-57
Bingo	Likes and Dislikes	69
True or False Search	Plans and Intentions	81-82
"Life" Gameboard	Regrets	95-96
NO WAY Game	Surprise and Disbelief	109
GO FISH	Worry and Reassurance	123-125

Questions, comments, or suggestions for new functions:
fiona@eslenglish.ca

Functionall Books

www.eslenglish.ca